The

COMING

JOBS

WAR

What every leader must know about the future of job creation

The
COMING
JOBS
WAR

JIM CLIFTON

Chairman of Gallup

GALLUP PRESS
1251 Avenue of the Americas
23rd Floor
New York, NY 10020

Library of Congress Control Number: 2011930933
ISBN: 978-1-59562-055-2

First Printing: 2011
10 9 8 7 6 5 4 3 2 1

To the girl at United Gate F4

TABLE OF CONTENTS

INTRODUCTION

The coming world war is an all-out global war for good jobs.

As of 2008, the war for good jobs has trumped all other leadership activities because it's been the cause and the effect of everything else that countries have experienced. This will become even more real in the future as global competition intensifies. If countries fail at creating jobs, their societies will fall apart. Countries, and more specifically cities, will experience suffering, instability, chaos, and eventually revolution. This is the new world that leaders will confront.

If you were to ask me, from all the world polling Gallup has done for more than 75 years, what would fix the world — what would suddenly create worldwide peace, global wellbeing, and the next extraordinary advancements in human development, I would say the immediate appearance of 1.8 billion jobs — formal jobs. Nothing would change the current state of humankind more.

The leadership problem is that an increasing number of people in the world are miserable, hopeless, suffering, and becoming dangerously unhappy because they don't have an almighty *good* job — and in most cases, no hope of getting one.

A *good* job is a job with a paycheck from an employer and steady work that averages 30+ hours per week. Global labor economists refer to these as *formal* jobs. Sometimes leaders and economists blur the line between good jobs (formal jobs) and *informal* jobs. Informal jobs are jobs with no paycheck, no steady work. They're found in, but not limited to, developing countries and include basic survival activities such as trading a chicken for coal. These jobs do create subsistence and survival, but not real economic energy. They are held by people who are not only miserable but, according to Gallup, suffering their way through life with no hope for a formal job — no hope for a good job.

Of the 7 billion people on Earth, there are 5 billion adults aged 15 and older. Of these 5 billion, 3 billion tell Gallup they work or want to work. Most of these people need a full-time formal job. The problem is that there are currently only 1.2 billion full-time, formal jobs in the world. This is a potentially devastating global shortfall of about 1.8 billion good jobs. It means that global unemployment for those seeking a formal good job with a paycheck and 30+ hours of steady work approaches a staggering 50%, with another 10% wanting part-time work.

This also means that potential societal stress and instability lies within 1.8 billion — nearly a quarter of the world's population.

It's against this backdrop that the coming jobs war will be fought. What's more, the big discovery that guides this book is that this new world war for good jobs will trump everything else. That's because the lack of good jobs will become the root cause of almost all world problems that America and other countries will attempt to deal with through humanitarian aid, military force, and politics. The lack of good jobs will become the cause of hunger, extremism, out-of-control migration patterns, reckless environmental trends, widening trade imbalances, and on and on.

My big conclusion from reviewing Gallup's polling on what the world is thinking on pretty much everything is that the next 30 years won't be led by U.S. political or military force. Instead, the world will be led with economic force — a force that is primarily driven by job creation and quality GDP growth.

If there was a U.S. Department of Job Creation and it was successful, its results would overwhelm the success of the U.S. Department of State or the Department of Defense. Political and military forces would no longer determine world outcomes.

The demands of leadership have changed. The highest levels of leadership require mastery of a new task: job creation. Traditional leadership through politics, military force, religion, or personal values won't work in the future like it has in the past. The nuances of personal values will be anchored in how they affect almighty jobs more than in Almighty God — or anything else. Human rights, stem cell research, gay rights, women in the global workplace — what will matter about these issues will be how they affect job growth more than how they affect family, political, and religious values.

Let me be as specific as possible in describing this new war. As of 2010, the world has a total gross domestic product (GDP) — or the sum of countries' total goods and services for one year — of $60 trillion. Of this, the United States has nearly $15 trillion or about 25%, which is huge. Over the next 30 years, the global GDP will grow to an estimated $200 trillion. So a new $140 trillion of customers, employees, new businesses, and equity will come into the global mix. The global war for jobs will be an all-out battle for that $140 trillion because within that sum of money is the next evolution of the best jobs in the world. Within that $140 trillion will rise the next economic empires, as well as the potential for societal hell.

World War II was a stunning military success that saved the world. Losing World War II would have ended America as the world knew it, not to mention much of the democratic Western world. It was a war for America's very freedom, for the West's freedom, for leadership of the free world. It was a war for all the marbles. Everything was on the line, and a loss would have changed everything.

The war for global jobs is like World War II: a war for all the marbles. The global war for jobs determines the leader of the free world. If the United States allows China or any country or region to out-enterprise it, out-job-create it, out-grow its GDP, everything changes.

This is America's next war for everything.

Chapter One

WHAT 7 BILLION PEOPLE WANT

More and more often, global leaders ask Gallup the same simple, yet colossal, question: "Does anyone know for sure what the whole world is thinking?"

Traditional economic data record an infinite amount of human transactions, from GDP to employment to everything everyone bought throughout their lives to birth and death rates. These data go to great lengths to indicate what man and woman are doing, but there is no ongoing, infinite, systematic account of what man and woman are *thinking*.

Global leaders are right to wonder. Every issue that keeps them up at night, such as poverty, war, the environment, unemployment/job creation, and extremism/terrorism, hinges on their constituencies' state of mind. What people think about — whether it's the economy, the Middle East, energy sources, or the environment — affects their behavior.

If leaders knew what the whole world was thinking — not just their own people — on almost all issues all the time, at the very least, their jobs would be a lot easier. At most, knowing what the world was thinking would make the work they do more effective. Leaders wouldn't make mistakes and miss opportunities because they misjudged the hearts and minds of their constituencies and the rest of the 7 billion with whom those constituencies interact.

It is precisely to make global leaders more effective why we at Gallup created a new body of behavioral economic data that represents the opinions of the world's 7 billion inhabitants across nearly every country and demographic and sociographic group imaginable. We call it the World Poll. We started it in 2005 and are committed to doing it for 100 years.

We knew going in that creating the World Poll was a monumental challenge, but it was even harder than we thought. To start, our scientists conducted stakeholder interviews with hundreds of world leaders and academics and combed through data from the best public opinion archives, universities, the United Nations, the World Bank, the European Union archives, the U.S. State Department — everything and everywhere they thought they might find existing information of this type.

What our scientists needed was a massively comprehensive poll of the world, and they couldn't find anything like it. So we made one.

The poll needed to cover almost every issue in the world, be translated accurately into hundreds of languages, and be meaningful in every culture. Even more difficult was engineering consistent sampling frames in more than 150 countries from Ecuador to Rwanda to Iran to Russia, Afghanistan, Ireland, Cuba, Lebanon, Kazakhstan, Venezuela, Honduras, China — you get the picture.

Having constructed the questionnaire, our experts found that their next biggest challenge was choosing a methodology that ensured consistent data collection to make the whole data set comparable. For instance, when we ask about life satisfaction, everyone from a Manhattan socialite to a Masai mother has to be asked the same question every time in the same way with the same meaning and in their own language so the answers are statistically comparable. We knew that it was critical to make the meaning of each question identical from language to language, culture to culture, year to year.

Furthermore, we needed to create reliable and consistent standards across the board so that leaders could see the trends and patterns. So we benchmarked wellbeing, war and peace, law and order, hopes and dreams, health and healthcare, suffering and thriving, personal economics, poverty, environmental issues, workplaces, and on and on.

Then our scientists and affiliated academics and colleagues from around the world who helped us make the poll got really busy. They counted and sorted and used every statistical technique known to man to analyze exactly what the world is thinking. The conclusions are complex. This may be the greatest understatement in Gallup's history, but it's true.

These data offer answers to many questions that could never be answered before. They make us intensely aware of how little we know about what is in the hearts and minds of 7 billion people and how often we are wrong about their hopes and dreams, their wills, and their ways of life.

As our founder, the late Dr. George Gallup, said back when the world had 5 billion inhabitants, "There are 5 billion ways to lead a life, and we should study them all."

THE DISCOVERY

Six years into our global data collection effort, we may have already found the single most searing, clarifying, helpful, world-altering fact.

What the whole world wants is a good job.

This is one of the most important discoveries Gallup has ever made. At the very least, it needs to be considered in every policy, every law, and every social initiative. All leaders — policymakers and lawmakers, presidents and prime ministers, parents, judges, priests, pastors, imams, teachers, managers, and CEOs — need to consider it every day in everything they do.

That is as simple and as straightforward an explanation of the data as I can give. Whether you and I were walking down the street in Khartoum, Cairo, Berlin, Lima, Los Angeles, Baghdad, or Istanbul, we would discover that the single most dominant thought on most people's minds is about having a good job.

Humans used to desire love, money, food, shelter, safety, peace, and freedom more than anything else. The last 30 years have changed us. Now people want to have a good job, and they want their children to have a good job. This changes everything for world leaders. Everything they do — from waging war to building societies — will need to be carried out within the new context of the need for a good job.

The word "good" is important. Some job, any job, isn't enough. When people talk about a good job, they mean a job that gives them the amount of work they want. Your cousin may pay you for helping out at his roadside food stand, but that's far from a job in a company that's officially registered with the government and where you have regular work for 30 hours or more a week.

The desire for a good job is the current will of the world, and whether or not you have a good job defines your relationship with your city, your country, and the whole world around you.

A great question for leaders to ask is: "Why is knowing that the whole world wants a good job *everything* to me?" The answer is:

Leaders of countries and cities must make creating good jobs their No. 1 mission and primary purpose because good jobs are becoming the new currency for all world leaders. Everything leaders do must include this new global state of mind or they'll put their cities and countries at risk.

- Lawmakers need to know whether new laws — such as taxes, healthcare legislation, and environmental regulations — attract or repel talented entrepreneurs. If enough talented people are repelled, then the new laws will cause brain drain and undermine job creation.

- Public school superintendents and university presidents need to think beyond core curricula and their graduation rates. Students don't want to merely graduate; they want an education that results in a good job.

- Military leaders must consider good jobs when waging war and planning for peace. They must ask themselves whether military strikes, occupations, or community policing will be followed by a growing economy with good jobs — or not. The opportunity to have a good job is essential to changing a population's desperate and violent frame of mind.

- Mayors and leaders of every city, town, and village on Earth must realize that every decision they make should consider the impact, first and foremost, on good jobs.

The evolution of the great global dream is going to be the material for hundreds of Ph.D. dissertations. But it's only the beginning of the story. Shifting the importance humans place on peace, love, food, and shelter — all the things people used to care about more than anything — to a good job suggests a significant change in the evolution of civilization. One of the most important changes is in global migration patterns.

Man and woman probably appeared about 200,000 years ago on the savannah plains in what is now Ethiopia. They fanned out to improve their lives, their tribes, and their families. And they have never stopped walking. The first to move have always been the boldest adventurers, explorers, and wanderers, and that's still true. Until rather recently in human evolution, explorers were looking for new hunting grounds, cropland, territories, passageways, and natural resources. But now, the explorers are seeking something else.

Today's explorers migrate to the cities that are most likely to maximize innovation and entrepreneurial talents and skill. Wherever the most talented choose to migrate is where the next economic empires will rise. That's why San Francisco, Seoul, and Singapore have become such colossal engines of job creation. When the talented explorers of the new millennium choose your city, you attain the new Holy Grail of global leadership — brain gain, talent gain, and subsequently, job creation.

You might notice how often I use America as an example in this book. That's not an accident. Though this book applies to every economy in the world — the science was tested and analyzed from a global perspective for a global purpose — America holds a special place in the global economy. Because it has a massive GDP and is a long-standing beacon for entrepreneurs all over the world, America has an economic and moral authority that no other country has.

That authority is eroding.

I'm an American and a patriot. But I'm also a realist. As long as the United States maintains its position as a global economic superpower, it also has the strength to advance a pro-democracy, pro-jobs, pro-free-enterprise world. Of the three, the most important is free enterprise because it is now the horse, and everything else is the cart. Over the past 100 years, capitalism has become the very basis of modern human development. Capitalism occurs where free enterprise — the freedom to create anything you want, to build whatever you want — is allowed to flourish.

I wrote this book with the belief that humans prosper and evolve most quickly in a culture, a community, or a nation where free enterprise is the core activity. Simply put, the exchange of goods makes everything else possible.

So while I use the United States as an example, I hope that readers from Buenos Aires to Budapest recognize the value that a job-creating U.S. economy holds for them. As a beacon of free enterprise — not the only one, certainly, but remaining the most powerful — America has a unique responsibility on the world stage. Everyone benefits from its success.

Chapter Two

JOBLESSNESS

America's most pressing current problem, according to Gallup, is a lack of good jobs. The country doesn't have enough good, full-time jobs for people who want work.

One might be led to think that America's most pressing problem is healthcare costs. It is not. It is a huge problem wrecking the economy and human energy, but it's not the biggest problem.

One might be led to believe that runaway government spending is the most pressing problem. It is not. It is a massive problem that will continue to erode the American economy for decades to come, but it's not the biggest problem.

One might be led to think that the most pressing challenge is global terrorism. It is not. It's a significant problem that needs a significant solution, but terrorism is not the biggest problem, not even close.

One might be led to believe that the most pressing problem is environmental degradation. It is not. The state of the environment is a problem that, if left unchecked, will destroy humankind, but not today, not even next year.

None of these problems matter when compared with the likely possibility of America slowly and then suddenly going broke — because none of these problems are so near. Going broke is what happens when there aren't enough good jobs.

So what would going broke look like on a national scale? Well, take a look at Detroit, and imagine that economic disaster coast to coast. Look at California. California can't pay its pensions, it will likely declare bankruptcy, a lot of its employees are going to be out of a job, and its bond holders won't be able to get their money. The same is true for Illinois and Michigan. Going broke means giving up and betraying promises. It means banks giving up on you and refusing to loan you and your business money. And it means selling things you hold dear.

America goes broke when its GDP falls and jobs can't be found. A country goes broke one company at a time and then one citizen at a time. It grinds down. And it's happening now. You and I, our friends and relatives, are going broke now because the United States of America is going broke.

All of this is happening because jobs and GDP live together, are the cause and effect of one another, and survive together and create one another. They are the chicken and the egg. So without significant, sudden GDP growth, America will not experience significant job growth. And without quick job growth, America will not experience meaningful GDP growth.

GDP in America is stalled, so it's not surprising that joblessness and underemployment have increased dramatically since September 2008. At this writing, the U.S. Department of Labor says that unemployment is around 10%. Gallup economics numbers are similar: unemployment is around 10%. But Gallup also looks at underemployment, and it is at nearly 20%.

Underemployment includes those who are unemployed and those who are working part time but want full-time work (underemployed). The U.S. government considers "employment" to include working for at least one hour during one week and being paid for it. So if I am an unemployed engineer and I mow your lawn, which takes me more than one hour, and you pay me $20, the government counts me as "employed" even if mowing your lawn was all I did that week. Gallup economics counts me as "underemployed" if what I wanted was full-time work, not an hour mowing your lawn.

Furthermore, if you want work and have stopped looking because you have lost hope of finding a job, the U.S. government does not count you as unemployed. Official U.S. government unemployment numbers are estimated using a survey of 60,000 households per month by the U.S. Census Bureau. Gallup's six categories of employment are estimated using a survey of 30,000 households per month. Both are accurate for what they intend to measure.

With that in mind, consider this: There are slightly more than 300 million Americans. Of the more than 150 million Americans who want a job outside the home, 15 million are unemployed, and 15 million are significantly underemployed. That's a total of 30 million Americans who don't have a good job. According to Gallup economics, of those 30 million, 18 million report having no hope of finding a job. Many of them also have no hope of paying the mortgage, feeding the kids, or buying gas to fuel the car to get to a job interview, and they have no reason to think things are going to change.

It's like 30 million Americans are fighting a war — a war for jobs — that they know they won't win. And the 18 million with no hope are the dead and critically wounded. They have lost energy, so they have dropped out of the battle for jobs, which is terrible for them and the economy. But worse, to a great degree, they've dropped out of life altogether: Joblessness is the strongest core driver of national hopelessness.

So while America experiences a decline in GDP, it's also experiencing a decline in a term you will start hearing a lot: gross national wellbeing (GNW). GNW is driven primarily by hopefulness or hopelessness.

When casualties of the jobs war give up hope of finding a job, just about everything else falls apart for them. They're much likelier to report being in bad shape on almost all conditions of health and wellbeing. They have more physical pain, experience more sleeplessness, are more likely to be clinically depressed, have more anger, and need more healthcare in general. People who have been out of work for 18 months or longer lose engagement in their network of friends, community, and families. The worst things in life start showing up when people experience extended unemployment.

But that's not all. These wounded will probably never fully recover. They won't meet their potential lifetime productivity and are likely to drift away from highly valuable community activities they might have once engaged in — coaching Little League, mentoring high school students, volunteering at the hospital, or leading support groups at church.

Every job loss permanently changes the relationship every individual has with his or her city and country — and subsequently, the culture. Twenty percent joblessness and 18 million people left hopeless structurally changes the social fabric of a country and creates a future it has to work its way out of, not unlike a huge national debt.

This recession will leave a more noticeable mark on American society than recessions of the past because "my job" defines "my identity" more than ever before. The wounds are different and deeper this time.

Clearly, having a good job is worth more than a paycheck. If you have a *great* job — one with unlimited growth opportunity, a manager who is interested in your development, and that gives you a sense of mission and purpose — you have about the best life you can have at this time in human history. Conversely, being unhappily out of work for six months — or even more deadly, being out of work for 18 months or more — is about the worst life you can have, anywhere in the world.

So why is it so hard to create jobs?

Jobs are the heart and soul of a nation, the thing that sustains everyone. Leaders know that. But almost nobody knows where or how jobs are created, especially those who think they know how to create jobs — the government, academics, experts from institutions of all types. Those people are usually the most wrong about job creation. They tend to dig in the wrong places.

THE CHICKEN AND THE EGG

GDP is a very important metric. It goes up when businesses are growing and customers are spending because GDP is the sum of all production and spending in one country in one year. Seventy percent of America's GDP is just consumer spending.

So if you run a business, you might think of GDP as top-line sales or total revenue. When GDP is growing, everything is going great because you're creating new jobs and increasing hiring. People have growing paychecks and pride in their work life, and everyone is spending. Everyone is exchanging goods and services of all kinds as fast as they can.

America's GDP growth increased for about 30 straight years, primarily because of a high-technology business-model explosion that was ignited by entrepreneurs and innovators.

But when GDP is falling, as in the worst recession in more than 60 years, everything goes wrong for workers. Businesses and organizations of all types reduce spending, stop borrowing, and stop sticking their necks out. They slash expenses to survive, including R&D, marketing, and advertising, and they institute hiring and travel freezes. Of course, jobs are eliminated, and people get laid off because organizations don't have enough money to spend on basics such as workers. Things get ugly fast.

That is where America is now. And it's likely to get worse. When it does, China is ready to take its place.

The United States has by far the highest GDP in the world. It has the biggest economy in the world. Few Americans know this. According to Gallup, 52% of Americans are more likely to name China than the U.S. as the leading economic power in the world today. This is a mistaken perception. If it were true, the mess America would be in right now would be incalculable. The U.S. GDP is nearly $15 trillion, and China's is almost $6 trillion. Although the gap is closing, the United States has an average annual household income of more than $84,000, while China's is just over $10,000.

TOP 25 NATIONS RANKED BY GDP:

1. United States $14.62 trillion

2. China $5.745 trillion

3. Japan $5.391 trillion

4. Germany $3.306 trillion

5. France $2.555 trillion

6. United Kingdom $2.259 trillion

7. Italy $2.037 trillion

8. Brazil $2.024 trillion

9. Canada $1.564 trillion

10. Russia	$1.477 trillion
11. India	$1.43 trillion
12. Spain	$1.375 trillion
13. Australia	$1.22 trillion
14. Mexico	$1.004 trillion
15. South Korea	$986.3 billion
16. Netherlands	$770.3 billion
17. Turkey	$729.1 billion
18. Indonesia	$695.1 billion
19. Switzerland	$522.4 billion
20. Poland	$470 billion
21. Belgium	$461.3 billion
22. Sweden	$444.6 billion
23. Saudi Arabia	$434.4 billion
24. Taiwan	$427 billion
25. Norway	$413.5 billion

I often ask seasoned executives, politicians, bureaucrats, and MBA students if they know America's current GDP, and amazingly, most of the time they don't. They almost never know China's or India's either, let alone that of Russia, Japan, England, Germany, or the EU. And about Africa, almost nothing.

Yet a country's GDP is its most important leading indicator. So goes its increase and decrease, so goes jobs, spending, tax base, and then everything else. Size matters, but so does direction. That's why this is an important fact: Looking at the U.S. and China, although the United States has a much higher GDP, it now has tiny GDP growth — about 2% a year. China has a much lower GDP, but its GDP is increasing at nearly 10% annually. That means unless there is a miracle, China will vastly exceed the GDP of the United States in less than 30 years; $6 trillion compounding over 30 years at 10% blows away $15 trillion compounding at 2% over the same period.

At that point, China will have the new world-leading GDP. China will have the new world-leading economy. China will be the new leader of the world, free or otherwise.

When the GDP lines cross, America's reign as the economic leader of the world is over. So are the designations of "place with the best jobs in the world" and "leader of the free world" because America will no longer have a disproportionate financial advantage that gives it the moral, economic, and leadership authority it has now.

This changes everything.

Leaders of other free countries, and not-so-free countries, will no longer defer to nor seek America's approval. They won't need to worry about U.S. moral authority or the consequences of ignoring it. They will look less and less to America for support because the U.S. won't have all the money and the biggest military. If the United States doesn't maintain its economic advantage, it doesn't have a trillion dollars per year to spend on national defense and general global security, which is more than the world's top 10 military budgets added together. The world will no longer defer to the United States for almost anything.

It has already started to happen in many places, such as Africa and Brazil, where they are beginning to look as much to China as to the United States for economic leadership. Imagine this suddenly being the case in every country, including Canada, Mexico, and Britain — all huge U.S. trading partners.

Less GDP growth also means that the United States won't have the money to afford its own national entitlements. It means that the math won't ever work on Social Security, Medicare, Medicaid, public schools, universities, local police and fire fighters, pension funds, and medical costs for millions of retired government workers, nor for building roads and bridges, critical R&D, and the never-ending races it has to win: the space race, technology race, medical race, and environmental race. All of it will slowly and then suddenly go broke because everything is tied to the almighty GDP.

When businesses and jobs fail, tax bases decrease, so the government has less tax money to support everything, and things deteriorate fast. It amazes me how few of my smart colleagues and friends don't realize that when businesses fail, a country fails. When businesses fail, jobs fail. When jobs fail, GDP fails. When GDP fails, institutions, infrastructure, and governments fail. GDP and job growth are the chicken and the egg.

America's only real solution — and keep in mind, this is true for every other country too — is to expand the size of the GDP pie. That means job growth. The bigger the pie, the more good jobs. Period. Most economists, liberal and conservative, will agree that this is the best solution. But America can't simply throw billions at innovation and hope for another breakthrough.

That's why and where Washington, almost all well-meaning politicians, and heads of state all around the world are wrong.

CUT BY A THIRD

To compound the problem, too many citizens are hallucinating. They think the government will come up with the money to save them. But the government doesn't have money. People and companies have money. And if the overwhelming majority of Americans aren't working outside of government jobs, America goes broke.

Until the last decade, the U.S. economy had unbelievable growth that disproportionately outpaced the rest of the world for 30 years. It also had a tax base that could pretty much cover everything. It could always pay for its needs and those of others. It could throw money at everything because America had colossal amounts of business profits and personal income to tax, which of course is the result of being overwhelmingly the largest economy in the world.

When the GDP falls, so does the amount of money the U.S. government has on hand to pay for everything because there is less to tax. The root cause is this: U.S. citizens aren't hatching new businesses, nor do they have the confidence to grow them, so the country doesn't have the new jobs that business typically creates or the income from them to tax.

Very few Americans are aware that small and medium-sized businesses are responsible for most of the jobs in America. Big businesses do not create significant numbers of new jobs. During the past two decades in the U.S., small and medium-sized enterprises have accounted for virtually all new jobs created. Jumbo-sized American businesses are very important to the economic ecosystem because they employ a lot of people, but mostly because they're the key customers of small to medium-sized companies.

The fact is that the rich tax base depends primarily on companies with fewer than 500 employees and even more so on companies with fewer than 100 employees. Small and medium-sized companies fund the great American way. Few leaders know this simple fact. So when small and medium-sized American businesses have no growth, there is no pile of money to send to Washington to cover the growing cost of services and entitlements.

As of 2007, there were about 6 million businesses in the United States with at least one employee; businesses with 500 or fewer employees represent more than 99% of these 6 million. There are slightly more than 88,000 companies with 100 to 500 employees and about 18,000 with 500 to 10,000 workers — and only about 1,000 companies with more than 10,000 employees. There you have it. That is America's new active military. So goes the success of these organizations — so goes the war for everything.

It is important to note that there are far fewer jumbo companies in America than most people think. Many tend to believe that America is run by "big business." But it is really run and dominated by small and medium-sized businesses.

So unless small and medium-sized businesses miraculously start up and grow like never before, the local, county, state, and federal government tax-base tanks and all the entitlements and government programs — thousands and thousands of them all across the country and states and cities — all will be drastically cut if they continue at all. Very soon, Social Security payments will need to be cut by a third; Medicare and Medicaid will need to be cut by a third; city, county, state, and federal jobs will need to be cut by a third; and the defense budget will need to be cut by a third.

This is where America is now. The pile of cash from taxes sent to Washington is about $2.6 trillion, and the amount Washington is spending is about $3.7 trillion.

Of course, there's a temporary way out of that mess — raise taxes way up. Americans are even willing to do it. Gallup finds that Americans would rather pay more in taxes than see their entitlements cut. But that solution has a flaw: If people and small businesses are paying higher taxes, although the government has more to spend, people and businesses have less to spend. When consumer spending drops, businesses have less to spend on expansion and hiring.

Gallup also finds that 47% of Americans endorse the idea of taxing the rich. This is not a long-term solution either. "Rich" is typically defined as having an annual household income of $250,000 and higher, depending on whom you ask. By and large, many of these "rich" people own or work in small to medium-sized businesses, not big business, and they reinvest their assets into their companies when their confidence is high.

They're using their money to keep their organizations running, which keeps their employees working, which keeps them spending, which keeps businesses functioning, which keeps the GDP growing. Raising business taxes drains the financial pool that should be used for creating jobs and for the R&D and investments that invent the stuff people want to buy.

And then there's this fact, which few people seem to recognize: All money is going to get spent anyway. You'll spend it, your business will spend it, or your government will spend it.

But be aware, any solution to job creation requires a lot of consumer spending or the GDP fails. America needs to simultaneously cut taxes and raise business output so there are a lot of jobs and everyone has money to spend at the mall, to fix up their home, to buy fishing equipment, and so on. A massive 70% of U.S. GDP is based on that consumer spending. So when consumers' take-home pay is reduced, by default, they lower their spending and subsequently lower the GDP.

And don't forget, small and medium-sized businesses are consumers, just as much as the guy buying a fishing pole. These organizations buy all kinds of things for their own businesses. So they are keeping 70% of the GDP energized as well.

This is the seminal point about job growth: Changing how the pie is cut doesn't significantly change anything. Governments can take more money from here and less from there, but in the end, there's not enough money. In any case, raising taxes too high doesn't create jobs.

Nor is it enough to reduce the government's super-bloated deficits and to halt runaway spending. Those things must be done before America drowns in costs and debt, but that won't create job growth.

What deficit spending *does* do is add fuel to a speeding train that ensures a more spectacular crash. This is exactly the track the country is on now as a result of huge entitlement costs and miniscule GDP growth to support them. America is currently staying afloat by creating more debt.

So if you receive a paycheck from the local, city, state, or federal government, you run a high risk of not only losing that paycheck, but also the promise that you will receive a pension plus benefits for life. A wide variety of government jobs and teaching positions in public schools are being cut as I write this. This is because tax revenues from businesses are shrinking as those businesses shrink.

Because most Americans don't understand this, you'll soon hear remarks like the following:

"My hard-earned government pension has been slashed." You'll start hearing this slowly at first, and then all the time. That's because when the GDP has no growth, there is no job growth, which depletes the once huge tax base that pays for everything. And so the government has to cut services by a third, including government pensions.

The more profit any company earns, the more investors make, and a lot of investors aren't people, they're retirement programs. When any company's value goes up, *everybody* gets a little safer and richer because everyone has a little money invested in everyone else. All money and jobs are closely connected. It's like oxygen — everyone breathes the same air. That's why the recession wiped out so many investment plans and shrunk U.S. GDP. GDP is like your sales or your checkbook. It has to outrun expenses or you go broke.

"No one is paying my parents' hospital bill." When GDP growth is stalled, the tax base that comes from small and medium-sized businesses shrinks. As a result, your parents can't have full, taxpayer-funded health services anymore. The government will have to cut these entitlements by a third. Medicare and Medicaid will cover much less, and the rest your parents will have to cover themselves. Things will only get worse when *you* are elderly.

"Who stole my Social Security savings?" If America no longer has the big tax base created by small and medium-sized businesses or the required ratio of workers to retirees to be solvent, it will have to cut Social Security by one-third. Of course, there has never been a Social Security "savings account," and Americans have never paid in anywhere close to the amount they collect. Many Americans believe that they have paid in an amount equal to or greater than what they receive in Social Security payments. But Americans pay in far less than they receive over a typical working career, and the remainder is funded by other workers. It is a transfer-of-income system, not a savings account. Currently, it takes about three workers paying Federal Insurance Contributions Act (FICA) taxes to support one retiree, and the system works as long as there is a ratio of three workers to one retiree. But it crumbles as the ratio of workers to retirees becomes, say, two to one.

With fewer jobs, there are fewer workers to fund Social Security. So payments get cut. And it's a significant problem for a democratic system that has elected officials who don't want to address it, because explaining that this program simply cannot continue making the payments the way it does now will cause them to lose elections. America's democratic system is easily the best in the world, but it is failing here.

Meanwhile, as America is shooting itself in the foot during the job wars, China has the United States in its sights.

Chapter Three

CHINA'S SURGE

Current economic predictions, with few if any dissenters, say that in the next 30 years, China's GDP will grow to a total far larger than that of the United States. As noted earlier, the total world GDP in 2010 was more than $60 trillion. Of that total, the United States has about $15 trillion, or what I will call a current global economic market share of about 25%. And China currently has a GDP of nearly $6 trillion, or a market share of about 10%.

You might be wondering how India and Russia will do. They might do OK, but they're starting too far back. India and Russia have GDPs approaching $1.5 trillion apiece. Almost nobody knows this because India and China are so often discussed in the same conversation, under the assumption that their GDPs are of similar size. Those who have been saying for 10 years that India is the one to watch, not China, are at least temporarily wrong. India might do well, but the country is getting routed by the Middle Kingdom.

Right now, China's GDP is more than four times bigger than India's. And it's more than three times bigger than Russia's and more than double Brazil's. Japan is close to China at slightly more than $5 trillion, but Japan's economy is even more stalled than America's. Germany is next at $3.3 trillion. The United Kingdom is just over $2 trillion, and France is just over $2.5 trillion — and they are both stalled. And to review, the United States of America's GDP is leading the world at about $15 trillion, but stalled, while China's nearly $6 trillion GDP is on a historic, world-order-changing run of nearly 10% growth per year.

Over the next 30 years, with total global GDP growth of approximately 4% annually, GDP will likely grow to a total of $200 trillion. Virtually all economists I've read predict that China's GDP will bounce to about $70 trillion by 2040 — a 35% market share of the entire world's economy. Those economists predict that the U.S. GDP will be growing at an average of 2.5% to about $30 trillion, or 15% global market share in 2040.

When and if that happens, America loses. The world changes; *everything* changes. China may dominate the world. But it won't have to use its military. When its GDP surpasses America's, it will dominate the world economically by a margin far more than the United States currently has. At that point, China will be the new leader of the world. All decisions between countries on the subjects of peace, trade, environment, borders, laws, and human rights would defer to China. Because more than ever, the new golden rule applies: He who has the gold, rules. And the country with the dominant GDP has the gold and the good jobs.

It's vital to understand all those GDP numbers because almighty jobs live in combination with GDP growth. Everything you just read will come true unless America gets its economic engine restarted and roaring. If not, it will slide into a new economic hell that few can imagine.

It might be hard to imagine, but there has been a preview of it in Detroit. If GDP and jobs continue to falter, a thousand big and little American cities will suddenly morph into a condition much like Detroit's. They will have declining city GDP growth. Small and medium-sized businesses will close. Big companies will have to be taken over by Washington or foreign owners. Any company that can afford to will leave. There will be massive layoffs and no jobs to replace them, huge unaffordable city debt, a decreasing tax base for the government jobs that support the community, and devastating brain drain. Houses will be bulldozed. There will be increased corruption among government leaders — a citywide economic hell.

Just a few decades ago, Detroit was one of the richest cities — and arguably the best city — in the world. It was a fantastic place to live and to run a wide variety of great businesses. But because of lousy local leadership and the rise of foreign competition, Detroit's businesses, government, and all its community support systems, including schools — everything came off the rails. And lousy top leadership creates lousy leadership further down the chain. America lost one of the best cities in the world because Detroit lost in the competition for jobs to Japan and Germany.

What went wrong with the macroeconomics of Detroit?

Most of the blame probably could be assigned to the car companies' short-sighted leadership, management, and vision; they managed as if the United States was going to be the undisputed world economic champion forever. They could make lousy cars because who cares? Everyone in the postwar world had to buy American anyway. Consumers had no choice.

The rest of the blame should be laid at the door of overly aggressive unions that knew they could have their way with the Big Three's weak leadership. Unions make the wrong people the customers. They create organizations almost solely for the benefit of employees, not the marketplace. Neither management nor unions had the vision to see how they were making their home city noncompetitive in the new war for GDP and jobs. That's the simplest summary.

$123,000,000,000,000

The idea of America turning into one big Detroit is not far-fetched when considering the prediction of the 1993 winner of the Nobel

Prize for Economics, Robert Fogel. He said that by 2040, the Chinese economy will be right at $123 trillion. That's more than three times the global economic output of 2000. China's share will be 40%, America's will be 14%, and the European Union's will be 5%. "This is what economic hegemony will look like," Fogel wrote in his article in *Foreign Policy*.

My own review of many economic calculations would say that Fogel was over-caffeinated as he ran his math, but he is a renowned and highly admired economist. In any case, virtually all the world's most credible economists have China as a prohibitive favorite by huge spreads to beat the United States over the next 30 years. Literally no economist I could find thinks the United States will win the upcoming economic battle of its life.

So even if Fogel is *close* to right, even if his prediction comes *almost* true, it will be jobs Armageddon in America. Its unemployment plus underemployment will rise to more than 40%. Leadership of the free world will not be just lost, but overwhelmed.

And that's the end for the American experiment in democracy. The history books will say it worked from 1776 to 2040 and then was overwhelmed by Chinese market-based communism.

Unless . . .

Chapter Four

UNLESS . . .

The United States will be overwhelmed by China unless there is an economic miracle. Americans are betting their entire country and the future of their children and their grandchildren on one big "unless."

Fogel, like many thought leaders, leaves room for that big "unless." "Anything's possible," he wrote. "An unexpected technological breakthrough could also shake things up." While his calculations cannot account for unforeseen world-changing inventions, it is more precise to say that his calculations cannot account for world-changing moments of rare entrepreneurship — because they aren't sensitive enough to detect the next Steve Jobs, Bill Gates, Meg Whitman, and Mark Zuckerberg or the next Apple, Microsoft, eBay, and Facebook.

What top economists' algorithms can't account for is exactly where America's hope for the future lies. And there is reason to hope. On some days, it seems impossible to me that this current economic nightmare can ever be fixed — but the nightmare has been fixed before.

Few thought leaders know this. America has been here before. *Exactly* here.

GERMANY AND JAPAN

More than 30 years ago, I was watching a panel of economists on TV, liberal and conservative, predicting that the United States would lose its global GDP lead, its economic advantage, to Japan and Germany. Based on what must have been simple regression equations, they could see that because of Japan's and Germany's growing manufacturing superiority, they would overtake America's leading economic position — especially Japan.

They predicted that the United States' growth would slow and that Japan's and Germany's would soar. As a result, America would fall to third in global GDP ranking, it would lose its global authority, and everything everywhere would change. German and Japanese leaders were downright giddy as they waited for their certain move to the top. One Japanese official made worldwide news by suggesting that Americans had become fat and lazy.

Of course, they were wrong. The United States didn't surrender its economic lead, and it jumped from an estimated destination of $3.8

trillion up to a staggering $15 trillion, a bigger lead than virtually anyone saw coming. Not only did the United States *not* lose, it jumped unforeseeably ahead in the creation of great jobs and GDP. America didn't fall to third; its GDP grew bigger than Japan's and Germany's economies added together. America grew at nearly five times the rate forecasted by the best economists.

The United States didn't fall into the stagnation and low growth so widely predicted. It grew its GDP, created good jobs, and actually strengthened its status as leader of the free world.

No one saw it coming. Virtually everyone was wrong, from U.S. economists to giddy Japanese and Germans.

America was such an underdog that its last 30-year economic victory was one of the country's least likely achievements. Yet you don't read, see, or hear this anywhere. It is not in history books, nor taught in MBA or political science courses. It was one of the most important wars America has ever won in 230+ years of existence — but no one talks about it, much less studies it. The Jobs War of 1970-2000, a tri-front war among the United States, Japan, and Germany was the war nobody covered nor recorded.

Nonetheless, the Baby Boomers — along with some significant Generation Xers — fought and won it. They commercialized Internet technology-based everything, created untold numbers of new business models around it, and then exported it everywhere. It was American entrepreneurship and innovation nobody saw coming that created millions of small, medium, and large companies — primarily small and medium companies — all over the country.

It was an unexpected 30-year economic boom that shot America to a 25% share of the whole world's economy that saved the republic almost as much, in its own way, as did winning World War II. If World War II saved the republic and democracy, the unforeseen technology-entrepreneurial boom that lasted from 1970 to 2000 re-saved the country economically.

The Greatest Generation saved America by beating the Japanese and Germans at war. The Baby Boomers saved America a second time by beating the same foes, Japan and Germany, in an economic war that determined the leadership of the free world, again.

So here America is in exactly the same place, except the experts predict that it's China the U.S. will fall to, rather than Japan and Germany.

What made the classical economists' predictions wrong more than 30 years ago was that their formulas and algorithms were limited. They couldn't see innovation combined with the entrepreneurship of thousands of small, medium, and big businesses sprouting up all around to create a historic run of GDP and job growth.

What that means is that one missing piece, *entrepreneurship and invention*, the one blind spot, the one *unless*, was more powerful than all the other variables combined in the economists' algorithm. That is a lot to think about. The traditional way of seeing the future failed to include the most important variable.

The traditional or classical economic formulas didn't work because the blind spot of unpredictable human entrepreneurship overwhelmed and washed out all the rest of the variables in the calculations.

That's not to say that Americans should pin their hopes on something rare, unforeseeable, and miraculous. They shouldn't cross their fingers and pray for another Internet to come along. What they should do is recognize the danger America is in — and the flaws inherent in projections from classical economics.

Predictions from classical economics cannot accurately detect the primary drivers of the future's thousands of potential outcomes. This is why classical economics was wrong 30 years ago and may be wrong again today. Classical economics has a central assumption that goes like this: "This is the math of the future according to the math of the past." Or: "This is the math of all past transactions of man and woman, so based on those, this is the future." It generally assumes everything keeps going like it is.

Usually it does. But sometimes it doesn't.

Chapter Five

CLASSICAL ECONOMICS VS. BEHAVIORAL ECONOMICS

Classical economics is the institution of data that records virtually every transaction of life. You are born, and someone writes that down. And then someone writes down everything else you do, especially everything you buy or sell in a lifetime — your visits to the dentist, your grades, your traffic tickets, every trip to the grocery store and mall and what you bought, your stock purchases, your vacations, your credit card purchases, your phone bills, the TV shows you watch — absolutely everything that can be recorded is.

Everything you transact during your life is recorded in the bottomless archives of classical economics. Finally, you die, and someone writes that down too, and that data point gets added to all the data points of mankind that record everything everyone "did." These are the numbers that rule everything.

Basically, classical economics is the science and institution of all transactions within a life, compounded over *all* lives. All that stuff makes up GDP.

The problem with using classical economics to foresee the future is that the most powerful predictors of GDP now lie within the fields of entrepreneurship and innovation. They are nearly impossible to see, let alone forecast. These blind spots hold more weight than what is visible. Within these blind spots are the most needed answers of all to this ultimate question:

What is the likelihood that there will be an unpredicted, transformational event that will cause a sudden extraordinary surge of entrepreneurship and innovation just like the one 30 years ago that saved America?

The answer to that question lies within behavioral economics.

BEHAVIORAL ECONOMICS

Behavioral economics represents a set of data that doesn't contradict but complements classical economics. What's most important to leaders is simply this: Behavioral economic data mathematically track what man and woman were thinking *before* they did something, *before* they transacted something. A state of mind, a frame of mind, an attitude, or a value is always in place *before* there is a transaction.

So the big leadership breakthrough within behavioral economics is to manage, lead, and build strategies and policies in the *before*, not the after.

Most academics define behavioral economics as the science of *choice*. Of course, everything people do during a day is based on what they decide. According to Princeton professor Daniel Kahneman, people make as many as 10,000 to 20,000 small moment-to-moment choices and a few big decisions every day — which email to send, where to sit, what to say, what to tweet, which taxi to hail, what to order for lunch, which TV show to watch, which house to buy, whom to marry.

Those mostly small choices create and determine all of an American's individual transactions, and when combined with the choices of more than 300 million other Americans, the total number of decision moments per day is right at 3 trillion. Just 3 trillion human "decision moments" per day for the entire United States. Multiplied by 365 days in a year, the annual total of America's small, medium, and large decision moments is roughly 1,000,000,000,000,000 — one quadrillion.

The science of behavioral economics is the mathematical quantification of the role human nature plays within those quadrillion moments of thought.

And then consider that all of an individual's decision moments are eventually connected to everyone else's around the world. And with Twitter, Facebook, LinkedIn, and on and on, those decisions and choices are more closely connected than ever.

So all of your thousands of daily choices, in combination with everyone else's, actually can change the course of your life and your country and the world. The whole world's population is connected by every person's state of mind.

Missing a bus doesn't change just your life; missing a bus now causes the rest of an interconnected world to change too. Years ago, I was booked on a flight that got delayed because of a major winter storm. I met a woman while I was stuck in the Chicago O'Hare airport at United Gate F4. It was a one-in-a-quadrillion chance meeting, and it changed our lives: We got married and had children who have all changed the world a little in their own ways. All because a flight got delayed.

A small decision to talk with a woman at O'Hare affected the rest of my life. Another small decision overwhelmed the whole Middle East. In December 2010, the local police chose to confiscate the vegetable cart of a 26-year-old Tunisian named Mohammed Bouazizi, which meant he could no longer support his family of eight. He went to the city's local headquarters to complain to officials who refused to see him. Soon after, Bouazizi set himself on fire in protest. The people of Tunisia took up Bouazizi's cause, and in less than a month, they ousted Tunisia's government. A few weeks later, Egypt was in revolt against its leadership, aided in no small part by an Egyptian Google marketing executive, Wael Ghonim. And Egyptian president Hosni Mubarak was thrown out. And thus a region-wide Middle East rebellion was born. This all started when a policewoman chose to confiscate Mohammed Bouazizi's vegetable cart and hence his job.

You change everything in the world just a little bit, sometimes a lot, as you make your thousands of decisions every day that create and cause millions of mini miracles in your own life and everywhere else. But there's no set of data that tracks this incalculably large phenomenon of "thinking" or "state of mind" just *before* you buy something, eat something, drive somewhere, make a phone call, go to church, get coffee, volunteer, coach a team, serve a customer, start a business, protest, or vote.

Classical economics can't analyze your state of mind well because it records after-the-fact transactions and outcomes. But leaders need to know those states of mind because what creates behavior is decision, and what creates decision is a state of mind or intent. And intent decides the fate of the world.

Intent is a force of nature, and it occurs before everything people do, before all those transactions that classical economists write down. Gallup is attempting to create new leadership metrics that measure intent through tracking polls and surveys of the behavioral economics of wellbeing — daily in the United States and annually across more than 98% of the Earth's population. This is the world's first and only comprehensive, systematic, ever-growing institution of data that records global behavioral economics. It represents the existing states of mind of all world citizens, from attitudes toward war and peace, job creation, innovation, wellbeing, global migration patterns, health needs, hope, community engagement, feelings of safety, availability of clean water, and food and shelter. This tracking technology establishes the standards of what the world is thinking on the 100 most meaningful behavioral economic issues we could find.

Collectively, there are infinite combinations of states of mind and thought patterns that occur before classical economics can record sales and transactions and subsequent contributions to GDP. Each of them is critical because each of them is wired to job creation.

THE NEW SECRET WEAPON

The core energy of entrepreneurship and innovation, the fuel for GDP, lies somewhere within the patterns and trends of these data. That's because core energy predicts the conditions that prevail before an economic storm hits, the conditions that occur before free enterprise creates growth and jobs. Simple states of mind, like confidence, optimism, determination, creativity, hope, and drive all exist *before* decisions that create the transactions of life. Those are the things that bring sudden GDP growth.

When leaders include the behavioral economics of the quadrillion decision moments of 300 million Americans in all their strategic leadership thinking, they change everything. The outpouring of human energy in one quadrillion moments creates surges in entrepreneurship and innovation, which in turn causes GDP and job growth to swell.

That's why behavioral economics is the new secret weapon for all leaders.

These quadrillion states of mind and decisions are the new power grid for American entrepreneurship and innovation and virtually everything that happens related to humankind's evolution. So go attitudes or frames of mind, so goes everything. This ever-present infinite combination of decision-making moments interacting with one another throughout the country and the world influences all national and global outcomes more than any other phenomenon.

Most leaders recognize that they have everything they need to start job creation right now. But very few leaders see the power in those decision-making moments. In fact, a lot of leaders think they can somehow buy job creation instead. But that won't work.

Sustainable job creation solutions can't be bought. Leaders can buy highways, bridges, dams, military equipment, and healthcare. But they can't buy — or rather, the government can't create — all of the new, sustainable jobs Americans need right now. Americans know what success looks like, but they can't demand it from the White House, from Congress, or from state or city governments.

That's because the miracle of real sustainable job creation lies predominantly within a combination of events and subsequently within human nature. As I said earlier, human development is the reason for and the outcome of free enterprise. That's why job creation isn't within the realm of government or any kind of top-down legislated solutions. Nor do good jobs come from cheap credit. Nor do they come from pouring billions into innovation only. But that's what leaders continue to do in America and around the world.

What if job creation is more likely to arise out of rare inspiration driven by the state of mind of more *freedom* — not a bigger credit line or more government stimulus for innovation?

Authentic job creation rises up out of human spirit, out of human behavioral economics. Look at it this way: Right now, many smart Americans are shrugging off the economic threat of China, telling themselves that no matter how well-educated Chinese kids are, no matter how big the Chinese domestic market is, no matter how healthy China's GDP is, America will win in the end because America can innovate better.

That's wrong. China has plenty of potential innovators. China's also pretty good at entrepreneurship. And the whole world knows that China is an excellent producer.

The one overwhelming advantage America has over China is that Americans have greater freedom. I doubt many leaders in China would dispute this. Americans are confident in, and faithful to, the country's brand of democracy. That faith in American democracy and things like America's freedom of speech, greater legal transparency, and tighter copyright protections make possible the free flow of ideas and unleash the power of one quadrillion moments of decision — even during bad economic times.

When national and/or city entrepreneurial spirit is high and resident engagement is flowing, breakaway GDP and job growth follow. When entrepreneurial spirit is low, when engagement disintegrates, everything stops. People lack the will to start new businesses. Small to medium-sized businesses don't have the confidence, spirit, or imagination to grow. Business stagnates, like it's doing now. Most politicians will say that banks aren't lending; according to Gallup, that is not true. Small and medium-sized businesses aren't asking for loans because they are not in a state of mind to stick their necks out and grow — because they lack confidence, because they don't have the spirit to grow.

It is the emotion of *lacking confidence* holding these businesses back, not a rational reason such as *lacking credit*. Classical economics can't help with this problem. Leaders need to take states of mind, measured by behavioral economics data, into account or there is no way out.

Classical economics assumes that everything people do is based on rational thinking. People buy something or make life transactions based on something rational, like money. Classical economics maintains that all decisions are predictable because man and woman are rational and impassive.

Behavioral economics says not so fast. It holds that man and woman are more irrational and emotional than rational when making life decisions.

For instance, why do people tend to sell their best performing stocks and hold their worst performing when they need liquidity? The answer lies somewhere in the fact that losing $100 feels worse than finding $100 feels good. Classical economics assumes that they would feel exactly the same.

From my review of decades of Gallup's research into behavioral economics, I have concluded that human decision making is generally 70% emotional and 30% rational. That's not to say humans are at the mercy of their emotions. Rather, they need to feel that conditions are right before they take chances.

So, if America is to be fixed quickly, it needs a minimum of 5,000,000 new good jobs right now and a minimum of 10,000,000 new good jobs, net gained, within five years. Those jobs can't be government-provided "shovel-ready" jobs because they have to be sustainable jobs created organically from the spirit of people through entrepreneurship and innovation.

And the entrepreneurs and innovators are building small businesses, not big ones. Gigantic companies tend to decrease jobs. This is OK because the jobs are lost via acquiring competitors and cutting duplication. This is actually healthy for an economy in the long run; big businesses cull one another's herds, maintaining Mother Nature's law of survival. Culling the herd is healthy, but it doesn't create new jobs.

Almost all new jobs are created by startups and small and medium-sized companies. Again, large companies are critical in the national free enterprise ecosystem because they are customers of the small to medium-sized organizations, including large and small social enterprises, and do almost all of the exporting.

ONE WAY OUT

But right now, the process is moving much too slowly. America's only way out, and there is no other way, is to get its GDP growing much faster than it is currently and to keep it ahead of, or at least comparable to, the rest of the world, especially China and India. That only happens when businesses, especially small and medium-sized businesses, start and *grow faster*. America will not have new good jobs in a thriving economy until GDP is growing at a minimum, consistent rate of 4.5% or more. This growth rate is enough for significant sustainable job creation, but it won't re-win the world.

Gallup has conducted deep advanced analysis on all the data from Gallup's U.S. and World Polls. We've studied all the macroeconomic data on job creation from virtually every corner of the Earth. We've analyzed all the material on the trends of world economics and consulted with the world's foremost thought leaders. Gallup is fairly sure that we have turned over more rocks and studied more data in infinite combinations — that we have watched more global game film than any institution in the world on the subject of job creation.

This is what I've learned from all of Gallup's work: America needs 5% GDP growth to maintain its leadership of the free world. It's enough to outlast China because that 5% is compounded off of a bigger number, and China has many serious problems to overcome. But that GDP increase will only come from the formation and growth of small to medium-sized businesses, not from anywhere else. Few leaders know this.

Yet, no one really knows how to create good, sustainable jobs, especially on the enormous scale I'm talking about that would get America's GDP booming. Worse, the enormity of the scale completely overshadows the individual — the man or woman who just wants a good job.

But here's the key: Individuals *are* the global economy. Every individual is a source of jobs energy in some way. Every individual is an economic engine. All the decisions people make every day *are* the economy. All the decisions and choices — yours and mine and everyone else's — are the economy. An economy rises and falls on people's combined consciousness. America's economic future isn't huge and vague; it starts with every individual. It's connected. It's changeable.

And the place to change it most surely, Gallup finds, is at the local level: in a city.

Chapter Six

CITIES

If you were to ask me, "From all the data you have studied so far, where will the next breakthrough, such as Internet-based everything, come from?" my answer would be: *From the combination of the forces within big cities, great universities, and powerful local leaders.* Those three compose the most reliable, controllable solution. Their combined effect is the most predictable solution to America's biggest current problem.

The cornerstone of these three is cities, especially America's top cities. All cities count and can contribute. But so goes the leadership of the top 100 American cities, so goes the country's economic future.

Of course cities, like organizations and workplaces, exhibit wide variation in economic outcomes. Austin has flourished, while Albany has declined. Sioux Falls is booming, while Sioux City is not. Think how different Detroit's outcomes are from San

Francisco's. Detroit went from being one of the most bustling economic cities in the world to one of the most spectacularly failed. One could even argue that citizens in San Francisco saved the republic and national job creation by leading the technology boom. One city is a drain on America, and the other continues to save it.

Globally, the variation between cities is even more defining. Consider the difference between Havana and Singapore. Lee Kuan Yew founded modern-day Singapore and Fidel Castro founded modern-day Cuba at about the same time and under similar circumstances. Singapore is now one of the most progressive modern societies in the world with a super-charged economy and great jobs; Havana is an economic and social disaster. One city worked, one city failed. The difference between these two is primarily the result of one thing: local leadership.

Fixing America's biggest problems and re-winning the world can only be accomplished one city at a time. Ultimately, all solutions are local.

Strong leadership teams are already in place within cities. A natural order is already present, in governments and local business and philanthropic entities. Every city has strong, caring leaders working on numerous committees and initiatives to fuel their local economic growth — let's call it the city GDP — and to create good jobs. The feat these leaders have to pull off is doubling their entrepreneurial energy by aligning all their local forces.

They succeed by declaring all-out war.

I don't use the term "war" lightly. This really has to be a war on job loss, on low workplace energy, on healthcare costs, on low graduation rates, on brain drain, and on community disengagement. Those things destroy cities, destroy job growth, and destroy city GDP. Every city requires its own master plan that is as serious as planning for war.

That plan must focus on the following:

1. *Recognize that the most important solutions are local.* Weak local leaders will look to Washington for more legislation and stimulus packages and more money for R&D to solve their problems. But what they need for job creation — entrepreneurs, enterprise energy, and the leadership to put it all together — is right there at home because cities are the highest probability source of job creation. In 2009, almost half of all venture capital money spent in America went to four cities: New York, Palo Alto, Seattle, and Sunnyvale. So the obvious question is: Why does the Bay Area create so much economic power and not Detroit? Both have the same federal government. They work under the same laws

and same rules. But San Francisco and Silicon Valley have created a culture that responds to innovation and creates business models like no other place on Earth. Cities that do this become a beacon for the most talented people in the world.

2. *Have your whole city wage a war for jobs.* Everybody in charge of anything needs to focus on job creation. If they divert their attention, vote them out. Be ruthless. If the bike path doesn't have anything to do with job creation, there is no bike path. If rezoning improves the jobs outlook, rezone. But not just any job will do — you want good jobs. The jobs war is won by knowledge jobs. Aim everything at those. The global economy is moving to the knowledge worker. You can build a slaughterhouse in your city, but that can't be the leading job strategy. Good jobs are created by entrepreneurs working with innovators creating a winning business model. The jobs war is what should get city leaders up in the morning, what they should work on all day, and what should keep them from getting to sleep at night.

3. *Align efforts citywide.* Every city needs a team to work on the alignment, focus, and strategies that put all businesses and local institutions of absolutely every kind on the same page. Meanwhile, the whole city has to be participating, highly coordinated, and working out of the same playbook to win.

4. *Don't allow your local constituencies to look to Washington.* Washington has something for you that is unsustainable or even worse, unhealthy. Free money eventually makes you more dependent. Free money, entitlements, more bureaucracy, less of your control — all these things make individual initiative, meritocracy, and free enterprise weaker and less competitive. To reenergize, to strike lightning on your city's GDP growth, its brain gain, its quality job creation, its vitality, and its future prosperity, don't expect national answers. "Everything is local" is truer regarding job creation than anything else. You have to jumpstart your city yourself.

In defense of Washington, it wasn't originally set up to be the nation's economic engine. The U.S. government has seeded whole industries through land grant universities, defense contractors, and scientific and medical researchers to name just a few. But the government has never, will never, nor should it be expected to ignite badly needed sustainable economic booms. These economic booms originate in the souls of individuals and great cities. Washington exists for law and order, war and peace, infrastructure, social services, and a wide variety of national and international policies that help hold the country together. But don't look there for sustainable, quality economic growth.

By design, Washington is bad at job creation. Free enterprise is arguably the biggest part of the *freedom* that the founding fathers provided. The U.S. government is good. It just needs the right expectations.

LOCAL TRIBAL LEADERS

All prosperous cities have a self-organized, unelected group of talented people influencing and guiding them — call them local tribal leaders. These are people who care very much about the success of their city: philanthropists, city fathers and mothers, business leaders, and other deeply invested citizens who get things done for the good of their city. Typically what's good for the city will eventually be good for the tribal leaders, but those leaders aren't purely motivated by self-interest. They do what they do for love of the city and the people who live there.

Local tribal leaders are loyal, highly successful, usually wealthy, respected, well-known people. It's not unusual to find them on the boards of several nonprofit organizations, often called "community foundations," where they meet and work to continually improve the city.

Tribal leaders are the opposite of "predatory elites," people with the power to rob their cities and countries blind for their own benefit. Tribal leaders aren't predatory because they aren't in it for themselves. Local tribal leaders care about the success of the whole community and all the people more than anything else in the world. They have immeasurable community loyalty, and for many reasons, they would never leave.

One of the best examples is Warren Buffett's loyalty to Omaha, Nebraska — not to New York or any other financial capital. He's been living in the same stucco house he bought in 1958 and has worked in the Kiewit Plaza for almost 50 years. He's been making a significant contribution to the economic wellbeing of his city for decades, and there's not a ghost of a chance he'll ever leave.

Tribal leaders include philanthropists, but not *just* philanthropists. These leaders give their time, money, and talent to the arts, programs for kids, the appearance of their city — all those kinds of charitable things, but what they really care about is that their city wins. For that reason, a lot of their time, money, and clout go toward the invisible things that help communities prosper.

Bear in mind, local tribal leaders do *not* include the people who are currently in office. A retired U.S. senator or a former, much-loved mayor might be a tribal leader, but primary among them are deeply involved legacy CEO types who run the biggest businesses and largest institutions; the university, hospital, and foundation presidents; successful local stars of almost any kind; and historically prominent families.

That's what makes tribal leaders a natural power source of economic growth. They know the people to talk to, they know the levers to pull, and they get things done. When they act together, they can accomplish things that *no one* else can. And they get them done better and faster than the city council can. Tribal leaders are typically more talented groups and have larger networks and more access to other talented people than the local government does.

If you need a new downtown YMCA building, the local tribal leaders can get it done. If you want to make a run at getting the next Special Olympics Games in your town, get the tribal leaders behind you. If you are recruiting a new technology firm to your city, you need the tribal leaders. If you are attempting to bring a new corporate headquarters to your town, or a pro baseball team, or a gigantic new tourist development; if you want more green space, a new airport, or a super-duper children's museum, you need the tribal leaders.

Your governor, mayor, and local area elected officials and city council will help, but they'll never have the same influence, money, connections, speed, or access to talent that the tribal leaders will. But regardless of how much local tribal leaders are doing in the top 100 American cities, it is not enough.

ONLY 10,000

Let's say there's an average of 100 city mothers and fathers per city in the top 100 cities. Naturally, there are far more than 100 in big cities and fewer than 100 in smaller cities. These numbers are generous, and some argue that each city, regardless of size, anywhere in the world, has only five. But I concluded that the number is significantly bigger in the new millennium than theories from the recent past would have it. That means that only about 10,000 people are leading and guiding an effort to create 5 million, then 10 million, jobs. It means that only 10,000 key players will determine whether the U.S. falls to China in leadership of the free world.

So if cities are the core of job-creating energy, "everything is local," and "so go the local tribal leaders so goes the soul of the city," then it follows that the future of the United States rides on the leadership success or failure of only 10,000 highly influential Americans. These are arguably the most important leaders in the United States because new job creation primarily depends on them. While 10,000 tribal leaders aren't very many people, they're the ones who will largely determine whether America recharges an economic engine the whole republic is counting on.

City councils, state legislatures, and all the elected officials in the United States are important. But cities need much more than what they can provide, and the tribal leaders should take responsibility for those elected officials. If you have a weak mayor, your city is going down. If you have mediocre city council members, your city is going down. If you have a humble set of leaders on your school board, your city is going down. If you have a group of near-unemployables on your state legislature, your state is going down.

When you see elected officials with little talent to lead in these 500,000 elected positions across the country and especially in your city, this is the local tribal leaders' fault. This is the fault of the local tribal leaders and all key local mentors in many walks of life for not being involved enough to push highly talented people to run for office. Plato made a very cruel but astute observation: "One of the penalties for refusing to participate in politics is that you end up being governed by your inferiors."

Here is the macroeconomic point. This is so simple. America re-wins the world by taking the country's entrepreneurship and innovation up a notch. But that can be accomplished only with the assistance of effective local tribal leaders. Americans have to read the game film right — and, as of now, they're not. Few people recognize the importance of cities, much less the importance of tribal leaders. If your city is failing, it is likely because you have weak leadership and little talent, commitment, and money resources from your tribal leaders. Talented and effective local tribal leaders are essential to cities. Their mentorship is essential to the people who create jobs.

SUPER MENTORS

The heroes America needs for this moment in history will come from those who guide, advise, encourage, and mentor a small business to success, which is the conception moment that saves a city and a country.

Here's an example. My late father, Don Clifton, taught at the University of Nebraska-Lincoln. In the mid-1950s, he conducted research on Reserve Officer Training Corps (ROTC) recruits that accurately predicted the success and failure of leadership candidates. The chancellor of the university took an interest in these results. Dad had no idea of the commercial value of his research until the chancellor called him to his office and suggested that if he built a similar test for identifying leaders for organizations, he could start a company.

Dad had immeasurable respect for the chancellor's advice, and his words gave him confidence and optimism. He went right out and started a company. It was a small business that did well. His company soon started adding employees and eventually created hundreds of jobs in his city. Thus, his organization became one of the thousands of small to medium-sized companies that made up

50% of America's total GDP and total jobs. It was triggered by one conversation and one super mentor.

Super mentors can be almost anyone, but they are not the innovators nor the entrepreneurs. They are the ones who light fires under the innovators and entrepreneurs. Super mentors are willing to take a risk for an individual and an idea. They are the tipping point of extra energy that causes the action to occur. They also encourage existing small and medium-sized companies to take risks. They do things like help entrepreneurs get a banker or a good lead, give advice, lend a hand or a shoulder at critical moments, and often join their board. That's an essential aspect of originating new jobs.

Super mentors create the almighty behavioral economic variables of confidence and action.

Our organization's founder, George Gallup, told me about the day he looked up from his desk and saw a young employee standing in front of him. The employee said that he thought Gallup should get into the advertising business. Dr. Gallup said that he was only interested in global polling but thought it was a great idea and that he would help. Dr. Gallup encouraged the young man to start the new ad agency in his office, told him to keep his typewriter, to get some clients, and then move to his own space once he got it going.

The young employee was named David Ogilvy, who went on to build one of the greatest advertising enterprises in the world,

Ogilvy & Mather. Dr. Gallup got nothing out of it. Dr. Gallup's only role in the founding of this now world-famous enterprise was to encourage, advise, and facilitate Ogilvy in his new entrepreneurial endeavor. No money or stock or fee — just mentoring, and just for the good of Ogilvy. For the rest of his life, David Ogilvy thanked George Gallup in speeches and writings.

And that's only one of more than 100 businesses Gallup employees have conceived and successfully spun out of this organization. But our numbers pale in comparison to those of businesses like IBM, which has incubated or stimulated tens of thousands of great organizations, including Microsoft and Intel. Today, Google is spinning out hundreds of startups. In total, highly inspired workplaces hatch literally millions of new startups. Low-energy, uninspired workplaces hatch virtually none.

Now, if you were to ask me to look at all the research and observations on job creation and find the most valuable American mentor over the last 30 years, my answer might surprise you. My answer would be Al Gore.

I would bet everything I have that there would have been no sudden $100 trillion surprise GDP growth over the last 30 years without a key facilitating moment by Al Gore. ($100 trillion is the sum of the total overages per year over 30 years of the big misprojected GDP for the United States.) This an example of government — while not creating jobs nor all-important business models — funding the germ of an invention that entrepreneurs could commercialize. And commercialize they did.

Here's what happened: Vinton Cerf is widely known as the "father of the Internet." While working in the DARPA Labs at the U.S. Department of Defense in 1972, Cerf and his collaborators designed the TCP/IP protocol, which was a way to get data to ride on telephone lines in packets, then on radio waves, and finally via fiber optic cables. It was the first big breakthrough in the invention that came to be called the Internet.

Cerf and his collaborators had set up their own Internet around the world, mainly for the purpose of defense communications. The Defense Department needed it because with Cerf's Internet, information could be transported to a safe place even in the event of things such as a world war, a natural catastrophe, or an attack on America's systems. This is the equivalent of the Wright Brothers getting their plane to lift into the sky at Kitty Hawk. That's why Cerf is widely known as the "father of the Internet." But the Internet's application was only for the Defense Department, and the rest of the world hadn't heard anything about it.

In 1986, then-Senator Gore went to Cerf's office and asked him what's new. When Gore learned what Cerf and his teams had made, he suggested that they share it with commercial types to see if they could generate uses for it. Cerf will tell you that he didn't completely see the merit in Gore's suggestion, as he couldn't see the immediate commercial value.

A bill was passed called the High Performance Computing and Communication Act of 1991, which has come to be called "The Gore Bill." It allowed this newly discovered technology within the Defense Department to be thrown out into the hands of business and industry — and the rest is world-altering history.

Imagine America's economy and world order if that simple conversation between Vinton Cerf and Al Gore had never occurred. What if something had stopped one of them — if a meeting got changed or a plane was cancelled because of weather. It was one of the quadrillion moments in which thinking and energy perfectly collided for Cerf and Gore.

What happened next, of course, is that a wide variety of dynamic entrepreneurs — Bill Gates, Paul Allen, and Steve Ballmer; Steve Jobs; Andy Grove; Meg Whitman; Michael Dell; teams at IBM and HP; and on and on — picked up the ball. A perfect combination of entrepreneurship and innovation went wild and saved America's place in the world.

America rose to new economic dominance and maintained its status as leader of the free world. The United States won the economic wars again in large part because of that one conversation, one meeting that connected rare historic inventiveness to commerce and enterprise.

With God as my witness, without that conversation between Cerf and Gore, there would likely be no Internet-everything technology that saved the U.S. economy and changed the world. There would have been no 30-year, $100 trillion GDP surprise overage. And the United States of America would have relinquished its global economic leadership, changing its way of life more than anything else has since its founding. American jobs were saved, and millions were created with the commercialization of the Internet and the businesses that sprang up around it.

That brings me to the central point: Al Gore's role. He wasn't the inventor of the Internet, nor the entrepreneur. Al Gore was a *super mentor*. He connected the inventors to the enterprise energy by getting a bill passed to make the Internet available to business. He saw something and took action when others didn't. He was the key facilitator.

To re-win the world's economy, America needs high-influence leaders who say, "Hey, that has value to commerce. Customers will want that. That invention could create a company or tens of thousands of companies. It could become an economic engine in our city for GDP growth and good jobs."

UNIVERSITIES

On a macro scale, cities with inspired workforces beat cities with uninspired workforces for job creation. And a city with highly talented local tribal leaders is essential for creating the jobs that will re-ignite America's GDP and save its economy. After cities and super mentors, there's only one thing left: the university. Universities are a critical part of new-company formation everywhere in the world, but America has a decided advantage. Why? Because America's top 100 universities are its most differentiating global strength in this war for jobs.

Great universities are the origin of most highly successful startups. Universities have, by design, the best ecosystem for entrepreneurship and innovation.

Super mentors are often university leaders, chancellors, presidents, and deans. A lot of super mentors are bankers (bankers are *extremely* important American business mentors), venture capitalists, private equity executives, and government leaders. A wide range of city leaders, often top executives and CEOs, and maybe most often, an enlightened influential family member are among the ranks of super mentors. But more super mentors of all kinds are highly involved and swirling around the top 100 universities in a wider variety of activities than anywhere else.

Many small and medium-sized companies get their international connections through universities. Top 100 universities always have friends and study partnerships throughout the world that can be used to help create customers and partnerships for exports.

Super mentors are not necessarily part of the faculty or administration, but they are engaged in activities, boards, and events of all types. This is why university/local business partnerships are so important to new businesses and job creation.

Many American cities have enough entrepreneurship and innovation talent to create a booming GDP and new jobs, but they lack the super mentors to trigger the all-important collision of matter that lies within enterprise and innovation. Roughly half of all ideas and entrepreneurial energy can be traced back to the top universities — not all of them, but half. I'd bet that the next hundred big breakthroughs, the ones that will save the economy and the country and create great jobs, are likely to originate in and around the top 100 American universities.

Universities are target-rich with inventions and smart business models and have a disproportionately high number of super mentors populating them. Consider that much of the explosion of free enterprise in the greater San Francisco area can be mapped straight back to Stanford and Berkeley.

The university system is a huge strength for the United States. Regardless of what you read, see, or hear, the overall university system in the U.S. has been and remains the best in the world.

There are many influential roles throughout American society, all of which are of critical importance and without which a country can't function. But at this juncture, whether the U.S. stays a world leader or even solvent will be determined primarily by three kinds of people: entrepreneurs, inventors, and super mentors. A prime foundry or petri dish of their energy and brilliance is the university system. And they're going to find greatness in a city, especially the cities that have active tribal leaders cultivating opportunities for free enterprise. So goes the entrepreneurial energy and mentorship within the national talent machine of the top 100 universities, the top 100 cities, and the most committed 10,000 local tribal leaders — so go the country's chances.

This is America's supercollider for sudden job growth.

Chapter Seven

ENTREPRENEURSHIP VS. INNOVATION

Nothing in the world can take the place of persistence. Talent will not; nothing is more common than unsuccessful men with talent. Genius will not; unrewarded genius is almost a proverb. Education alone will not; the world is full of educated derelicts. Persistence and determination alone are omnipotent. — Calvin Coolidge

Please read this next section carefully so you do not misinterpret this dangerous material. And if you happen to misinterpret it, you wouldn't be the first. The whole world has it backward.

Here it is: Innovation is not rare in America. Neither is creativity. In fact, there's an *oversupply* of innovation in America and other places in the world.

There's nothing wrong with that. What's wrong is that America — and most all countries — have a mass shortage, a significant undersupply, of *successful business models*. Many innovations fail to successfully commercialize. The scarcest, rarest, hardest energy and talent in the world to find is entrepreneurship. Call it rare salesmanship, call it genius business-model design, call it rainmaking, but whatever the case, America doesn't have enough to fight the coming global jobs war.

World leaders — especially American leaders — and city leaders are spending the majority of their time and billions of dollars on innovation. They're digging in the wrong place in their frantic search for quality GDP growth and job creation because they're concentrating almost solely on innovation.

What the U.S. needs more than anything in its quest to win new good jobs in its cities is that rare talent to start companies or to create business models that work, that grow organizations — big ones, small ones, medium-sized ones, sustainable ones.

The sweet spot is in the small to medium-sized business realm because these companies create and grow far more jobs than jumbo companies do. Jumbo corporations are good for everybody because they support the full ecosystem, but they don't create many jobs. Regardless, the economy needs them all. America needs — the world needs — millions of new small, medium, big, and jumbo organizations.

But regardless of the size of the company, *the business model really is everything*. Innovation has no value until it creates something a customer wants. Here is a Gallup economics finding that few leaders anywhere know: Even the best ideas and inventions in the world have no value until they have a customer.

Last year, I attended a meeting at the National Academy of Sciences in Washington, D.C. A group of leaders and CEOs of the biggest government and university labs in the country told me that they have inventions — some as big or bigger than the Internet — now on their shelves, done and ready to go. The most advanced, sophisticated labs in America, and thus the world, have an oversupply of discoveries, breakthroughs, and inventions gathering dust because they don't know how to turn them into something customers want. When and if someone does commercialize them, America's next big run could be bigger than the last.

The business model is everything, at least for the next 30 years, because there are no new sustainable jobs until there are new customers. That's true for corporations, nonprofits, churches, schools — every organization you can name.

This is not to diminish the importance of innovation. It's just that innovation has little to no value until it joins with entrepreneurship. Innovation itself doesn't create sales. Entrepreneurship is the driving phenomenon within the city supercollider. The precious connector between innovator and customer is the almighty entrepreneur: the person who envisions a value and a customer and then creates a business model and strategy that create sales and profit.

People usually think of entrepreneurs as those who start businesses, and as such, entrepreneurs are vital — absolutely necessary for humankind. But what pushes humankind forward, as well as entrepreneurs, are "intrapreneurs." Intrapreneurs work inside companies and are the brains and energy behind creating customers. They're usually marketing and strategy people, often rare salespeople, but these intrapreneurial breakthroughs can come from any corner of a business.

So when people say "entrepreneur," they should always include the intrapreneur. An entrepreneur/intrapreneur is the individual and her team who create the business model that subsequently creates more customers, more demand, more product build-out, and then the miracle of quality GDP growth and authentic job creation.

Business models, free enterprise, and innovation drive one another. Historians and weightlifting instructors can tell you that human development occurs when there's resistance. Humankind doesn't evolve, biologically or culturally, without resistance. Survival of the fittest can be cruel, but it is absolute and necessary. That's what I've got against socialism: It reduces the necessary resistance; it takes tension and even fear of loss away, thus making people and organizations flabby and complacent. Capitalism and customers create resistance, and from that, human development. Humans have to win. That's competition; that's opposition and resistance and survival — and competition creates customers, and customers create jobs. This is the core concept that caused capitalism to trump socialism.

Gallup recently won a significant new client project. The project was for $6 million per year. I called our COO and asked her how many new jobs it would create. "Fifty," she told me.

If you were to ask me, "From all your research, what is the best predictor of new jobs?" my answer would always be *new customers*.

Too many American leaders try to draw a straight line from money to jobs. Or R&D to jobs. Or investment to jobs. Or government stimulus to jobs. Business and government leaders throw money at everything under the sun except the most important target: creating new customers. The more they throw money in the wrong directions, using mistaken premises, the worse they make everything.

What leaders should be looking for — and are not finding because they're digging in the wrong place — is the individual and her team who have the rare talent to build a great and growing corporation, regardless of size, who can take something that's of value to someone else and find a way to sell it.

The ultimate issue with any new enterprise is almost always whether it has attracted a leader with enough sales or rainmaker talent to create customers. Regardless of whether the institution is a business, a social enterprise, a charter school, or a new government program, the real power comes from the enterpriser, not the innovator, the thought leader, or the idea itself. The enterprisers are far scarcer than the rest.

Many venture capitalists and government-funded programs fail because a big or little idea by itself remains still and lifeless until enterprise energy finds it. Venture capitalists and federal program leaders disproportionately and overwhelmingly bet on the cart, not the horse. When the project fails, the group typically says, "We lost our funding," never, "We failed to generate enterprise energy."

Once again, let me say that innovation is vital. America has to out-invent the world. But that is a given. The country has to invent about one-third of all big inventions. And this is something America is good at: The United States has successfully invented and commercialized between 30% and 40% of all breakthroughs worldwide, throughout virtually all categories, in the last 200+ years.

But please allow this chapter to record that, unless primary emphasis is put on the key attribute of entrepreneurship, an untold number of world-changing inventions and ideas will die. These are inventions that could re-win the world for America, but the world will never know them because they were never brought to life with entrepreneurial energy. And again, the good money and good jobs come from the business model, not the invention.

What was really spectacular about Vinton Cerf and his team's invention wasn't just the TCP/IP protocol, but rather the way American enterprise adapted it into magnificent commercial products that are fun and useful. It improved human lives and advanced human development similarly to how the wheel and flight did.

It was not the invention of the Internet but the commercialization of the Internet that advanced America and the world, not unlike the transistor, an invention that also changed humankind. But until someone got interested in how it could create billions of customers, the transistor was just another technology sitting on the shelf — so was the Internet.

Entrepreneurship has a direct impact on supply and demand, but with a distinction: It doesn't just provide supply, it *builds* demand. Entrepreneurship alters the supply-and-demand equilibrium. That's why it's crucial to mentor budding entrepreneurs, not just people who want to work alone or be their own boss. True entrepreneurs build new jobs and increase overall demand and spending because they bring something new to the game. Either they take a current product or service and make it available to those who are not served or who are underserved, or they take a new idea and build enthusiasm, interest, and desire for it — a new demand.

An example: Henry Ford didn't invent the automobile. He invented a way to manufacture and sell automobiles to middle-class people. Without Ford's entrepreneurship, cars would be useless to most people. Ford didn't just move jobs around, he built a whole new demand for cars.

AN INVENTOR'S STRENGTHS VS. AN ENTREPRENEUR'S STRENGTHS

I mentioned that the world is digging in the wrong place for the key to job creation. To find the right place, the world needs to know the psychological traits inherent in inventors and in entrepreneurs.

World-class inventors and entrepreneurs are alike in that they're extremely driven, competitive, and passionate about something. Those are the similarities. But let's look at the big differences.

An inventor is a creative and purpose-based problem solver looking for better ways to do things. Inventors create *discoveries and breakthroughs*. An inventor or innovator might be a highly trained scientist or simply an extremely talented thinker, blessed with heavy doses of God-given creativity and intellectual talent. Inventors almost always have a deep passion for improving something. Inventors are rare *thinkers*.

An entrepreneur, on the other hand, is a person of action, one who possesses an unnatural overload of two attributes: optimism and determination. Because entrepreneurs are optimistic, they don't see barriers; because they're determined, they never quit. Individuals who possess extreme amounts of optimism and determination *get things done*. Entrepreneurs are rare *doers* — and because of this, they are the most valuable people in the world, at least as far as the pursuit of economic development, GDP growth, and almighty job creation are concerned.

ENTREPRENEURS WITH HUMBLE IDEAS

One of my favorite entrepreneurs is Wayne Huizenga. He has had, in my opinion, three humble business ideas in his career.

When he was a garbage collection manager, he decided to build his own trash collecting business. That was a bad idea because the world didn't need another trash collection company. Trash gets picked up pretty well. But nevertheless, he built his own trash collection business. And he turned it into a great multibillion-dollar worldwide organization, a Fortune 500 company, and a leader in environmental sustainability that was profitable and valuable to its customers, a great place to work, and an international powerhouse. You have heard of it: Waste Management, Inc.

The question is: Was it the idea or Wayne that made Waste Management such a successful American enterprise for tens of thousands of highly engaged employees and that created good jobs of all kinds? Most global thought leaders would believe it was Wayne's *good idea* more than his *entrepreneurship*.

Wayne's next idea was arguably worse. The big idea was to rent movie videos through branded outlets, malls, and small free-standing buildings. It didn't sound very good to me — and I did much of the research on it for him. That became his second multibillion-dollar Fortune 500 company — Blockbuster, Inc. And Blockbuster, too, was a great American organization that created millions of customers and a hundred thousand new jobs.

And with that, Wayne did what no one had ever done before: He created *two* Fortune 500 companies in one lifetime. Was it the ideas that made them Fortune 500 companies and great places for thousands of people to work — or was it Wayne?

Then he had one more bad idea: a national chain of used car outlets. He called it AutoNation, Inc., and it became his third multibillion-dollar Fortune 500 company.

So what explains these staggering successes: the innovation or Wayne? This is a really important question because whatever idea Wayne chooses seems to become a *good* idea. The predicting variable of success in Wayne's case is "Whatever idea Wayne chooses is a good idea because he makes its business model work." It is not "Wayne is good at picking innovative ideas."

But most thought leaders still believe it's the second answer.

My hunch is that if you took away everything Wayne has — all his financial resources, management team, money, keys to his car — and put him in a one-bedroom apartment in downtown Miami, a multibillion-dollar Fortune 500 company would likely burst out of that room. Because of his extreme optimism, his unstoppable determination, and his incredible energy, Wayne is able to build hugely successful enterprises, and he doesn't need a breakthrough innovation to do it.

It is wiser to study the person than the idea.

Another favorite American enterpriser of mine is Ted Turner. A 24-hour news channel didn't seem to be that good of an idea to me. I did initial market research on 24-hour news as well. No one wanted more news, and the news Ted was going to show was just a reel of reports played over and over again. Trust me, so I don't have to go into a long review of the research, 24-hour news is a mediocre idea. It was far from the invention of the airplane or the transistor or the discovery of the Van Allen radiation belt. It is right there with the "breakthrough" idea that banks should extend business hours past midafternoon so that people who work during the day could actually use them.

Ted Turner, of course, built CNN, a famous, high-mission, highly profitable, multibillion-dollar worldwide TV enterprise out of a small business in Atlanta from a very humble, hardworking idea.

But Ted Turner has optimism and determination bursting out of his whole body, so whatever idea he picks becomes that next "great idea" in broadcasting. His energy just needed a host. It found 24-hour news, old movies, and sailing.

His newest innovation is buffalo ranching. Honestly, buffalo ranching and a chain of restaurants that serve buffalo meat. That is a really bad idea. There can't be a person in the world who would say, "Oh my gosh, I wish I had come up with that one." This is a horrible idea that Ted will most likely make work because whatever idea he chooses becomes the lucky host for his unstoppable optimism and determination. And along with his success come thousands of great new jobs for highly engaged workers.

Let me review one more really dumb innovation: an Internet site where people can sell junk to one another — a sort of 24/7 worldwide garage sale. In my opinion, this is the worst of the worst. This innovation gets my vote for "An idea that will never ever, ever work."

Nonetheless, Meg Whitman chose to lead that innovation. It's called eBay.

Not only is eBay one of the great new highly profitable technology companies of the last 25 years, it has also created thousands of great new jobs and income for millions of customers who trade on eBay's system. It is a free-enterprise colossus. Although eBay may be a humble idea, Meg made it great because whatever idea she chooses has a high probability of being a success of world-beating importance because she makes it work.

Meg's rare optimism and determination will always create a lucky host. And thousands of even luckier workers found great jobs at eBay because of her.

Is it innovation or entrepreneurship? It is both. But the key insight here is that innovation by itself has no value until it is chosen by talented entrepreneurs.

Entrepreneurs are rare, however. While America will not win without inventing a third of everything, the country should focus first and disproportionately on world-class entrepreneurship because that's what creates jobs. Lots of people have good ideas, but most new businesses fail. It's not for lack of passion, but lack of customers. There are millions of new businesses launched every year, each creating a handful of jobs, but only few of them take off because most didn't have the unstoppable determination and optimism required to win.

This is what to look for in an entrepreneur: somebody with an idea that totally consumes him — an idea that becomes the way he thinks, a way of life, and an obsession. That obsession fuels unstoppable optimism and determination. All businesses have terrible problems, but highly talented entrepreneurs enjoy the problems, even welcome them. Untalented entrepreneurs are destroyed by these problems. That's why just wanting to be an entrepreneur isn't enough. Encouraging people to be entrepreneurs the usual way — just take a class, get a loan, and then you're ready — is setting them up to fail.

America needs to understand the talent makeup of people who start companies. Right now, Gallup is looking into it. The implications are huge for institutional investors. In the new economic climate, investors will have to ask which they're investing in: the individual or the idea.

With uncanny accuracy, educational psychologists can rank an auditorium full of students on their innate ability to learn. SAT or IQ tests signal high-potential learners in science, math, language, technology, engineering, and medicine. But if you asked these same educational psychologists to rank these same students by innate capacity for entrepreneurship, they'll probably have no idea how.

Some leaders even believe that anyone can be trained to be an entrepreneur. This is a mistaken assumption. Entrepreneurs have a rare gift. My estimate is that for every 1,000 people, there are only about three with the potential to develop an organization with $50 million or more in annual revenue.

Yet while the educational system has nailed the process of developing the best learners, America is still in the dark about cultivating gifted enterprisers. This could explain why there is such an oversupply of innovation and an undersupply of entrepreneurship. America has overdeveloped the more controllable trait and left the more mysterious trait's development to chance.

Chapter Eight

HIGH-ENERGY WORKPLACES

There are currently more than 6 million companies operating in the United States. Within these workplaces is the will to create the next 20 million businesses. Many startups are incubating within these existing organizations. They will manifest themselves either when intrapreneurs create new business models in their own companies or when entrepreneurs venture out and start new firms of their own. America needs both. Every city in the world needs both.

Let me summarize the biggest body of behavioral economic data in the world on workplaces. It comes from a Gallup study on workplace productivity, and it consists of 12 critical elements of work life. Gallup has asked millions of workers worldwide to respond to these items for more than a decade and always finds the same thing: Miserable employees create miserable customers.

That may seem obvious, but try to find solid metrics in any organization that clearly link employee misery to customer outcomes by individual work unit. Every company has solid-gold data for sales and profit or product defects, but few know their misery quotient by workgroup.

And if you can't find the misery quotient, I guarantee your accounting department will. It will take a year or two though. I've observed that employee misery precedes all the easy-to-find data by one day to two years, depending on the type of business. Somebody in the company needs to treat a customer like hell for between one day and two years before the customer will defect. Customer defections are immediately followed by job loss.

But as I said before, few companies know their misery quotient. And not nearly enough organizations in the world have the metrics on the intricate behavioral economic wiring between customer and employee by work unit. This information is rare because leaders are drawn to all the wrong metrics, so they pay attention to all the wrong things — they ask employees questions about compensation, benefits, vacations, parking, and the cafeteria. Virtually all employee surveys lack statistical correlations to sales increase and subsequent job creation because they ask the wrong questions — directing leaders to work on the wrong things.

DEFECTIVE EMPLOYEES

For all you Six Sigma enthusiasts, a miserable employee, particularly a miserable manager, is a defect — a defect for the company, the customer, and ultimately the country. Gallup counted the number of extremely miserable employees — which we refer to as "actively disengaged" because they also encourage others to be disengaged — right at 20 million nationwide. Out of approximately 100 million full-time workers, there are 20 million actively disengaged employees in the United States.

Re-winning the world's best jobs is part of winning the innovation and entrepreneurial wars. And as America wins those, initially it will be manufacturing its own inventions, at which the country will *temporarily* be the best in the world. But shortly thereafter, far cheaper labor in other countries is likely to take that over.

That is OK, as long as the United States incorporates the invention, creates the almighty business model, and owns and operates it around the world. This simple U.S. world trade and economic strategy works in many productive ways now (think iPod). This whole premise depends on Americans' ability to be innovators, to be entrepreneurs, and especially to create world-class business models to ignite authentic GDP growth and job creation.

Low-energy workplaces, or as Gallup calls them, disengaged workplaces, will derail that.

Where is the United States on the behavioral economic standard of miserable vs. engaged employees? Right now, as I mentioned earlier, the country has just over 100 million employed people in real full-time jobs. Gallup has determined that 28% of the American workforce is "engaged," another 53% is "not engaged," and a staggering 19% is "actively disengaged."

The 53% of *not engaged* workers are not hostile or disruptive, and they are not troublemakers. They are just there, killing time with little or no concern about customers, productivity, profitability, waste, safety, mission and purpose of the teams, or developing customers. They're thinking about lunch or their next break. They are essentially "checked out." Most importantly, these people are not just part of your support staff or sales team. They are also sitting on your executive committee.

And then there are the 19% of *actively disengaged* employees who are there to dismantle and destroy your company. They exhaust managers, they have more on-the-job accidents and cause more quality defects, they contribute to "shrinkage" — as theft is politely called, they are sicker, they miss more days, and they quit at a higher rate than engaged employees do. Whatever the engaged do, the actively disengaged seek to undo, and that includes problem solving, innovation, and creating new customers. When you're in a meeting with nine other people, odds are that two of them are taking notes to make damn sure whatever you're planning doesn't see the light of day.

The 28% of *engaged* employees are the best colleagues. They cooperate to build an organization, institution, or agency. They are the creative force behind everything good that happens in an organization. They are the only people in your organization who create new customers.

The explosion of entrepreneurship that GDP growth requires won't happen until the country doubles the number of its engaged employees — just doubles it, especially in the sweet spot of job-creating small and medium-sized businesses, but really in every company. If companies double their number of engaged employees, they'll double the number of ideas and commercial energy running through the national grid of interconnected workplaces. If that happens, America will grow the best jobs in the world.

For more than 75 years, Gallup has counted, sorted, and analyzed every state of mind imaginable in the workplace. And we found 12 behavioral economic-based standards — 12 frames of minds — to which virtually all performance outcomes can be attributed. We didn't find 45 or 80, but 12, all separate and distinct from one another.

Gallup also found that other apparent key variables (such as "I'm fairly compensated") outside the 12 didn't distinguish between engaged and disengaged employees. These 12 items hold up statistically throughout all job variations and throughout business and industry, retail, hospitality, manufacturing, government, nongovernmental organizations (NGOs), the military, education — virtually all jobs everywhere in the world.

Employees' responses to the 12 survey items neatly factor all workers into the three categories of engaged, not engaged, and actively disengaged. These items are:

Q01. I know what is expected of me at work.

Q02. I have the materials and equipment I need to do my work right.

Q03. At work, I have the opportunity to do what I do best every day.

Q04. In the last seven days, I have received recognition or praise for doing good work.

Q05. My supervisor, or someone at work, seems to care about me as a person.

Q06. There is someone at work who encourages my development.

Q07. At work, my opinions seem to count.

Q08. The mission or purpose of my organization makes me feel my job is important.

Q09. My associates or fellow employees are committed to doing quality work.

Q10. I have a best friend at work.

Q11. In the last six months, someone at work has talked to me about my progress.

Q12. This last year, I have had opportunities at work to learn and grow.

A great manager has employees who score all 12 of these items as highly as possible; the items are measured on a 1-5 scale of agreement, with 5 being highest (or "strongly agree"). All innovation, entrepreneurship, authentic sales growth, new customers, job growth — all the things that every company needs most — are sparked and inspired by the relationships between managers and employees that these 12 items measure.

As I said before, if twice as many American workers scored high on these 12 frames of mind every day, that would create sudden significant change; it would generate more rapid job growth than anything else. Going from 30 million engaged workers to 60 million engaged workers would change the face of America more than any leadership institution, trillions of stimulus dollars, or any law or policy imaginable.

Raising the percentage of America's engaged employees from 28% to 60% would double innovation and double entrepreneurship. It would create the conditions necessary to suddenly overwhelm competing nations because engagement creates new customers.

Is this doable, or is it a pipe dream?

Actually, Gallup sees these types of dramatic increases in engagement all the time. We have studied millions of people in hundreds of thousands of workgroups in companies and countries all over the world. We have seen companies double engagement, or even triple it.

Recently, Gallup conducted a meta-analysis, looking at 199 research studies across 152 organizations in 44 industries and 26 countries. Within each study, Gallup statistically calculated the business/work unit level relationship between employee engagement and performance outcomes that the organizations supplied. In total, Gallup studied 32,394 business/work units including 955,905 employees with a close look at nine outcomes: customer loyalty/engagement, profitability, productivity, turnover, safety incidents, shrinkage, absenteeism, patient safety incidents, and quality (defects).

Gallup found that workgroups in the 99th percentile of our employee engagement database have nearly five times the odds of having above-average performance at their jobs as those in the 1st percentile. When compared with bottom-quartile business units, top-quartile units have 12% higher customer metrics, 18% higher productivity, and 16% higher profitability. These top-quartile units also have 37% lower absenteeism, 25% lower turnover (in high-turnover organizations), 49% lower turnover (in low-turnover organizations), 27% less theft, 49% fewer safety incidents, 41% fewer patient safety incidents, and 60% fewer quality incidents (defects).

So, yes, it's doable. If every organization in the United States doubled employee engagement, America would once again surprise the world, just like it did during the dot-com boom. The United

States would win by doubling the human energy that drives entrepreneurship and innovation.

Companies, government offices, schools, factories, and every workplace in the country need to double the number of highly engaged employees or they put America's competitiveness at a disadvantage. Doubling national engagement is not a pipe dream because large and small organizations are doing it now. And by doing so, they are creating more customers and more exports.

The game-changing resource in the workplace lies within the almighty power of human nature (behavioral economics) first and the almighty dollar (classical economics) next. And that resource is the engaged worker — but it is in her brain and her entrepreneurial energy, not in her hands. The potential for discoveries, breakthroughs, trillions of dollars of authentic revenue, millions and billions of dollars for your organization, millions of authentic jobs and subsequent real GDP growth in the United States — is in a worker's state of mind.

And the potential for using human imagination and determination will remain unlimited. Technology is exploding because human development has caused it to explode. As Thomas Edison said, "We don't know one-millionth of one percent about anything." And that's absolutely true of maximizing human potential too. But fortunately, we are learning something about behavioral economics.

THE GALLUP PATH

There is a definitive set of elements that traces the steps of the role human nature plays in any organization. We call it The Gallup Path. Gallup identified this set of elements from our database of employee and customer interactions, including 500,000 separate international business units — the most advanced analytics ever on the subject of behavioral economics.

Let me walk you through The Gallup Path, starting at the top.

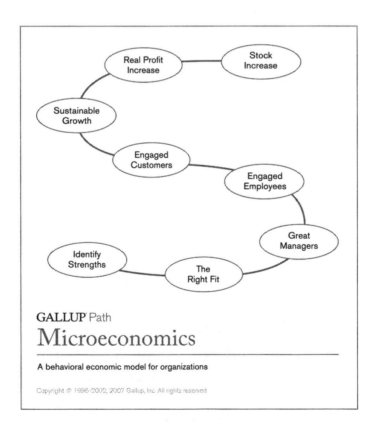

GALLUP Path

Microeconomics

A behavioral economic model for organizations

Copyright © 1996-2002, 2007 Gallup, Inc. All rights reserved.

Publicly traded corporations aim for profit increase because it is the single biggest driver of stock increase. When companies have profit and stock increase, everything else is wonderful. Everybody's job is safe. Leaders are heroes to shareholders and the press, and they get bonuses. The company can invest in growth activities, increase R&D, create products and internal startups, open offices around the world, acquire companies, make increased contributions to retirement and pension funds, spend time and money on community needs, and continually nurture the next generation of leaders because what the company does works and wins.

When profit and stock prices are increasing, a company can push enormous amounts of positive energy through virtually all economic networks, especially in its hometown because it is closest to the power source. Meanwhile, that business sends large sums of tax money to its city, state, and federal governments. And because the company produces so much economic energy, it can sponsor endless charities and social initiatives throughout its city and state. It can make its city vibrant and attractive to everyone who lives there while employing some of the world's best workers and attracting more. To some degree, a little or a lot, every individual and every organization of every kind benefit when any organization's profit and stock are growing.

That's because successful local companies are not just engines for job creation but also engines for local social and community improvement. Community organizations, one way or another, are funded by small, medium, and large businesses. Successful companies with big profits drive rich local social capital.

Few leaders are aware of this, but when there's an increase in the profit and stock price of HP, Ann Taylor, Apple, Google, Walmart, Harley-Davidson, or thousands of companies you and I have never heard of, to some degree — either a tiny bit or a whole lot — everyone is affected, whether you are a direct stockholder in the company or not. Every business success ripples throughout the entire economy.

What role does behavioral economics play in this? Profit increase predicts share increase about 80% of the time. Real sales growth predicts profit increase about 80% of the time. Keep in mind that there are many ways an organization can achieve profit increase: by implementing a huge cost-cutting Six Sigma or lean management program, for instance, or restructuring the balance sheet, or using generally accepted accounting principles, or announcing a new product or a key acquisition. All of these methods increase stock price, but authentic, sustainable profit and stock growth are most likely to occur as the result of real sales growth, especially when that sales growth is organic. Organic growth is better than acquired growth for job creation, for example, because mergers and acquisitions destroy more jobs than they create.

If you like predictive statistics, your next question is surely "What leadership activity or behavioral economic variable best predicts real sales increase?" The answer is customer engagement. Gallup scientists call it customer *engagement* rather than customer *satisfaction* because "feeling satisfied" doesn't reliably predict buying more and doing it more often. Being *engaged* is a better predictor of sales growth.

The big finding is that when customer engagement increases, sales increase. If a customer rates his partnership with your organization as a 5 on a 1-5 scale versus a 4 or lower (most executives believe a 4 is a good score, but it isn't), he'll do three things that less engaged customers won't:

1. Buy more frequently

2. Spend more per visit

3. Pay a higher margin

American businesses need to have the highest customer engagement scores in the world because when they do, they win the hearts and minds of all U.S. customers. And then, slowly but surely, they win the hearts and minds of all global customers, just like McDonald's, Cargill, Starbucks, IBM, and others have done. If they don't, all U.S. businesses will slowly and then suddenly be taken away, just like the Germans and Japanese took away the auto industry.

The global customer race is not unlike the space race. To re-win the world, U.S. companies have to be first in the customer race like

America was the first to put a man on the moon. Winning all the best customers in the world would be a "man on the moon" moment for the United States. Winning customers may not actually require *manufacturing* all the products for them, but it does require the best inventing, designing, engineering, strategies, financial tools, global logistics, leadership development, advice, education, and the almighty business models too.

Winning customers means keeping entrepreneurship, innovation, and workplace energy way ahead of the rest of the world, as well as leading the world in infinite discoveries and applications. You get the picture. America needs to *own* global customer intelligence and then work its strategies back from there — owning the business models first and then aiming everything at the highest quality GDP growth to create the best jobs in the world in America.

Working down The Gallup Path, as customer engagement drives sales growth and stock price increase, employee engagement drives customer engagement. You can find the most powerful energy that you can push through your company in the intersection of employees and customers — not either one alone; the energy is in the intersection.

You have to have great products, great marketing and advertising, great traditional economics in general, but the most powerful behavioral lever to pull is increasing the number of employees who are engaged. When you have engaged employees, you get a predictable domino effect: engaged employees create customer engagement, which creates sales growth, which creates profit increase, and finally, that creates stock increase. And then, everybody wins.

STRENGTHS-BASED LEADERSHIP

To make all of this work perfectly, organizations must focus on the strengths — the ability to provide consistent, near-perfect performance in a given activity — of every employee. Not the strengths of the organization, but the strengths of each individual.

That is why The Gallup Path begins with "Identify Strengths." If you get this one right, all of your employees' talents and strengths will be well-matched with their roles, which is essential for doubling employee engagement.

If you've identified the strengths of your employees, you won't make an introvert into a salesperson and ask him to make cold calls or try to turn an ADHD marketing rep into a bookkeeper or an extreme individual achiever into a manager. Once you have tested an employee, interviewed her, and chosen to hire her, you must give her a job that fits her innate talents or the potential of The Gallup Path will never be realized.

There's one behavioral economic demand left, and it is big. If you don't get this one right, everything after it falls apart. Once you have carefully diagnosed an individual's strengths and given her that near-perfect job that she has real talent to perform with a mission and purpose, make sure she has a great manager. Everything else on The Gallup Path shuts down if an employee has a bad boss.

If you do give her a great boss, one who cares about her development and growth, then you have successfully engineered the basic domains of running a high-energy, behaviorally driven organization with unlimited potential. There are no limits to what your organization can become as a human power plant in your city and as an economic engine for GDP and job creation.

ONE BIG COMPANY WITH 100 MILLION EMPLOYEES

A leader's most defining moment is the decision of whom to name as manager at any level — whom to put in charge of developing the talents and skills of others. If a leader chooses good managers, everything works. If a leader assigns the wrong person as manager, everything fails. Nothing fixes bad managers, not coaching, competency training, incentives, or warnings — nothing works. A bad manager never gets better.

Scale that leadership math up to the entire U.S. workforce with its more than 100 million real full-time jobs, and here is how it might play out: Every job role tends to have a ratio of one manager per 10 employees. So if America was one big company, then it has 100 million employees, 10 million supervisors, and 1 million managers of those supervisors. Just 1 million managers determine whether America wins the world's workplace for everything.

The problem is, according to Gallup economics estimates, nearly one in five U.S. managers are dangerously lousy, which is a conservative estimate. If you were to ask me how U.S. workplaces can beat China's workplaces, my answer would be, "Fire all lousy managers today." Replace them with good managers. If they are lousy at developing people and leading teams, fire them. They will never get better. If you won't do it for your business, do it for your country.

Getting the right managers in place is the most critical moment of talent engineering throughout an entire society, not just labor markets. More money, jobs, and GDP turns on who is named manager than on any other decision.

You might wonder how the United States, as one company, made it this far. It's because until recently, the United States and the European Union enjoyed moderate competition, even effective monopolies in some cases, throughout their regions and the world. Car companies, electric companies, TV networks, airlines, and many other businesses enjoyed near-monopoly status for a long time, especially in the 1960s, '70s, and '80s, depending on the industry. There was no competition from China, India, or Korea.

People and their potential have not mattered as much in the past, not until globalization really started to kick in. Managers and teams probably weren't as responsible for the success of companies in the 1990s and especially in the 1970s and 1980s as they are now.

Surviving the upcoming global war for jobs requires a new demand of managers. They must be masters at understanding the role human nature plays in all outcomes and at maximizing human potential, or America can't win the war for everything.

Hence, the new profound role of behavioral economics in all leadership.

Chapter Nine

CUSTOMER SCIENCE

To win the jobs war, America needs to be the best in the world not only at entrepreneurship and innovation, but also at customer science. The country simply cannot win new jobs unless it uses the most advanced sciences in the world to create billions of new global customers.

Simply put, new global customers create new U.S. jobs. That's why America needs to more than triple exports in the next five years — or continue on a downward slide. The battle for global customers will be the defining element in the new war for jobs and GDP growth. Whoever sells the goods and services, and whoever owns the companies that own the customers, wins. The United States needs to average a minimum 10% annual increase in exports over the next 30 years to maintain its leadership of the free world.

The big advantage China has over the United States right now is that China wins customers with low prices. This strategy really can work — not great, but OK for a while — because as long as America invents the new products and innovations, it can produce them for the first iteration and create millions of great jobs. But when China evolves to understanding customers and their needs better than U.S. companies do, the United States loses its advantage.

If America allows China — or India or anyone else — to get further into behavioral economics and customer science than it does, the country will lose the jobs war. That is what Toyota, Volkswagen, and other automakers did to U.S. car companies. They won by simply listening to customers better and then delivering what customers wanted at fair prices. America cannot afford to concede the science of customer insights or customer-centric innovations to China or any other foreign competitors or it risks losing to them. This is a "game over" moment for America.

Why? Because if those countries learn to provide better service and meet customers' needs better, then customers won't need U.S. retailers and supply chains to deliver products. China will set up its own retailers and supply chains, and God help America if that were to happen. Its best retailers, shops, banks, car dealers, restaurants, grocery stores, malls, and even movie theaters would be Chinese owned and controlled, which means that the best cash flows, margins, and stock values all become foreign owned.

There has already been a trend lately toward foreign-business takeovers, and the effects have been economically and psychologically devastating in headquarter cities. Belgian-based conglomerate InBev bought American icon Anheuser-Busch. When that happened, a little bit of St. Louis died. Brazilian-backed 3G Capital acquired Burger King, and a little bit of Miami died. When a national oil company in Venezuela bought out CITGO, a little bit of Houston died. When the Arcapita Bank, formerly First Islamic Investment Bank, bought a majority of Caribou Coffee, a little bit of Minneapolis died. No question, when foreign companies take over American businesses, something changes. Americans feel somehow that they're not what they used to be.

This might sound controversial to some Americans, but they should all love Walmart, no matter what particular beef they might have with the company. If it weren't for Walmart eating up all the little corner grocers and hardware stores, the Germans, Japanese, French, and for sure the Chinese would have. Somebody will come do it better. Walmart, Target, and Costco should be applauded for leading the way in reinventing retailing in America because if they hadn't, foreign companies would have. Right now the big box stores are worried about the "dollar stores." That's great — Americans want Americans competing against other Americans.

The flip side of great performers like Walmart, Target, and Costco is poorly run companies. They're job killers, especially in their headquarter cities. Local firms, big or small, that are bad with customers will be cannibalized by outside companies. The most dangerous outside companies, as far as your city is concerned, are foreign. Jobs appear in combination with customers and GDP growth and then again in combination with American ownership and control.

You might think I'm an advocate of protectionism. I am not. Quite the opposite, I am 100% pro trade, pro competition, and pro law of the jungle. By no means do I think America should erect barriers against foreign-owned companies.

The solution isn't to avoid competition, but to take it head-on. Americans have to know more about American customers and all customers in the world than Europeans do, and especially more than the Chinese, Brazilians, and Indians do. The country that best knows the needs and preferences of all 7 billion customers will have a prohibitive advantage in winning the world's best jobs.

Sure, companies should do a great job of executing Six Sigma, lean manufacturing, reengineering, TQM, and so on. These practices all work and are essential to winning, but they are no longer enough. I don't know about your organization, but Gallup has squeezed the last drop out of most of these brilliant practices, all to its great benefit. But the low-hanging fruit of improving processes and efficiency has all been picked. What remains untapped is the incalculable opportunity within the emotional economy of customers.

In fact, one of the biggest blind spots in most American businesses is that they don't realize how big the emotional economy is within their own customer base worldwide. The best corporate leaders in the United States are still unaware that they are leaving a great deal of money on the table through abysmal execution of the employee-customer links because they are so focused on the "hard numbers," of which they have already squeezed every dollar to diminishing returns.

You and your teams can double and quadruple exports and foreign sales by increasing the number of your current customers who give you a 5 for partnership on a 1-5 scale. Let's assume that 20% of your customers give you a top score, which is about the global average. By raising that number to 40%, you will experience record sales increases without spending a nickel more on advertising and marketing. You grow, America grows, jobs grow.

From my 40 years of studying customers, this represents the biggest missed opportunity of all organizational leadership — probably because it is easier for leaders to talk a good game and then at the end of the day, just cut their price, falling back to the rule of classical economics that every decision is rational, which is not true. What customers at any level really want is somebody who deeply understands their needs and becomes a trusted partner or advisor. The business world fails at managing this one most critical behavioral economic variable more than any other, but it remains the lowest hanging fruit for organic growth for virtually all businesses.

Leaders have yet to learn that relationships trump price in almost all business circumstances, from hair salons to high-tech consulting. He who most deeply understands the customer's needs tends to win and always gets the highest margins. That's why talent and relationships can almost always beat low price — they inspire customer engagement. To measure customer engagement, these are the best 11 questions Gallup scientists have found to ask customers anywhere in the world:

CE1. Taking into account all the products and services you receive from them, how satisfied are you with (Company) overall?

CE2. How likely are you to continue to do business with (Company)?

CE3. How likely are you to recommend (Company) to a friend or associate?

CE4. (Company) is a name I can always trust.

CE5. (Company) always delivers on what they promise.

CE6. (Company) always treats me fairly.

CE7. If a problem arises, I can always count on (Company) to reach a fair and satisfactory resolution.

CE8. I feel proud to be (a/an) (Company) customer.

CE9. (Company) always treats me with respect.

CE10. (Company) is the perfect company/product for people like me.

CE11. I can't imagine a world without (Company).

If America doubled the number of engaged customers — those who respond with a 5 on these statements — worldwide, it would secure its economy and more than triple exports.

Gallup economics has also determined the standards for customer engagement as they apply to business-to-business (B2B) companies. These items have been the most predictable metrics of global customer sales increase:

- (Company) has a clear understanding of our business issues.

- (Company) has had a significant impact on our business performance.

- (Company) is an easy firm with which to do business.

- I consider (Company's) representatives to be trusted advisors.

PHIL AND PHIL

Here are two real-life examples that illustrate the power of understanding customers' wants and needs. In one case, the company had a clear strategy for understanding customers and selling value over price; in the other, the critical emotional connection essentially happened by accident. Both examples have implications of hundreds of billions of dollars of real revenue growth and job creation.

A few years ago, the division president of a large telephone company called me. She offered to replace our current Gallup long-distance lines for a quick 10% savings. This meant a lot of money to us. And the telephone lines we need in the United States and around the world are a commodity. They all seemed to work well and sound fine, regardless of the long-distance carrier we used. As we are an employee-owned business with serious employee owners, it seemed an easy decision to dump our longtime partner for one offering a significantly lower price.

I called our top managers in the IT department, Phil and Phil, and they said they would study it. They soon got back to me with their recommendation to stay with our current technology partner — Partner A. Phil and Phil are super-competent technology leaders at our company, and I was sure that they would have a great explanation.

Phil and Phil described in detail the innovations that Partner A has brought to the table over the past few years, including a deal-saving technology breakthrough that helped us rescue one of our best accounts, a large and demanding retailer. They felt that Partner A brought more to the table than just global lines. This partner helped us win, save, and grow accounts.

Phil and Phil reported that Partner A knew our industry as well as or better than our own people. They also informed me that Partner A was reengineering our global teleconferencing and building a new state-of-the-art interviewing system throughout the European Union that would quickly make us the technology leader in our field in the EU. And they were in the middle of helping us compete to win a complex project in Brussels.

Partner A perfectly executed an organic growth strategy. Such a strategy succeeds when companies maximize relationships with current customers. So, though 10% across the board is a lot of money, the advice-based relationship Partner A brought us was a lot more valuable.

MY NEIGHBORHOOD BOOKSTORE

In the next example, things didn't look like they were going to turn out so well and did so only by accident.

When my son decided to go to law school, I went to my local bookstore in Georgetown to get the *U.S. News & World Report: America's Best Colleges.* This is a major bookstore, with three stories of books, escalators, a big music department, and a Starbucks coffee shop. I looked all over the store and couldn't find the college report. The staff person I checked with was on the phone to a friend and was ever-so-slightly put out to be interrupted. "If it wasn't where you looked, we don't have it," she said, and then went back to her call. Suddenly, it felt like everyone in the store was unhelpful.

Naturally, I decided to leave — and never come back. I really wanted to picket the place. As chance would have it, a skinny, 15-year-old-looking kid with a bookstore ID tag caught me as

I headed for the door and asked, "Is there something I can help you find?"

He didn't have the greatest retail personality in the world, and he didn't pretend to. He didn't say, "It's great to have you here." He said, "Is there something I can help you find?" He not only got wound up helping me find my college guide, but he also found a book that was more precisely what I wanted — a book specifically about law schools. He was grinning because he not only found what I was looking for, but he helped me discover that there was another book that better met my needs.

Then he asked, "Is there anything else I can help you find?" I asked if he was familiar with the book *The United States of Europe*. He said he was, and it was excellent. I told him that I don't like to read hardcore academic books. He guaranteed me that this wasn't. In the end, I bought two books I didn't intend to purchase, and we looked at some others I eventually came back to get.

Though my trip to the bookstore started out poorly, it turned out to be a perfect example of organic growth, in this case by chance. Three outcomes were possible when I walked in the store. The bookstore staff could do a lousy job and sell me nothing, which damn near happened. They could do a good job and sell me exactly what I came for. Or they could do a great job by discovering what I really wanted, which was information about law schools, and by advising me to buy something else I wanted that I didn't even know was available — then following up by asking what else I needed and recommending another great idea. Purely by chance, the third option happened when I ran into that helpful skinny kid.

I left the store enthusiastic and feeling victorious about my new books. My clerk was genuinely enthused because I had taken his advice, and we became acquaintances. I always seek him out at that store, and I've never again considered picketing the place.

The difference between lousy, good, and great is money — a lot of money.

This bookstore chain has about 1,000 stores; let's say 1,000 people like me walk in each of them each day. That makes 1 million moments of customer engagement per day times 365 days per year. In other words, 365,000,000 customer moments when behavioral economics counts.

If each moment puts about $50 on the line, that would mean that this bookstore chain has an emotional economy of around $18 billion beyond its business goals, which are essentially "order taking." This bookstore chain has sales of about $10 billion. Its missed emotional economy is larger than its total revenue. The problem is that the bookstore is at risk of getting into financial trouble, not keeping up with the times, and eventually being wiped out by foreign competitors. This serious risk exists because — if the experience I had in the store before running into that helpful skinny kid is any indication — it is lousy with customer centricity and customer insight. A bookstore chain cannot thrive and succeed if it depends on random encounters with helpful people.

Management practices like Six Sigma would have said to just take the college report order and charge $10 for it. And missing the $10 sale is a "defect." Well, yes it is. But a bigger missed opportunity is not understanding and outfitting the individual customer's real reason for being in the store, which has unlimited possibilities.

MORE EXPORTS

The truth is that all companies are leaving a fortune on the table. That money represents what customers wanted and got — or didn't. If Americans mismanage their companies' behavioral economics, foreign businesses will break them or take them over. Any time an American company is lost to a foreign company, like Anheuser-Busch to InBev, Coors to Molson, or Chrysler to Fiat, all American flags should fly at half-staff.

Again, I'm not suggesting protectionism, but the opposite. I am suggesting that Americans should be highly aware of the importance of U.S. ownership, local headquarters, and control over the best companies in the world. Maintaining ownership and control of all organizations and enterprises headquartered in the United States matters more than ever in the new global competition for the best jobs.

Creating good jobs is about reaping the infinite benefits of global competition and partnerships. Extreme capitalism has outrun extreme socialism for one reason: meritocracy and competition accelerate progress and human development. Extreme competition and extreme meritocracy are America's friends. And the ultimate customer-centric act for any small, medium, or large company is exporting. Any leadership team of any company that finds a global customer and then creates exports to that customer are American heroes.

The math of the solution is this: American small, medium, and big business needs to increase current exports of about $1.5 trillion 20 times over the next 30 years. I know that sounds impossible, but so did putting a man on the moon. America can do this if it understands that winning the majority of the world's customers is doable. It is simply a matter of having deeper customer insight and centricity at the core of all short-term and long-term strategies.

But is America's next generation up for the 30-year tournament for everything? That's a serious question. The answer is found in the U.S. public school system. Its students are the new incoming players, and that fact alone is cause for alarm. Almost 80 million of the country's next innovators and entrepreneurs — its talent source for the future — are sitting in a K-12 classroom right now.

Chapter Ten

K-12 SCHOOLS — WHERE ENTREPRENEURS ARE CREATED

There are more than 75 million students enrolled in schools in the United States — nearly 50 million in the 5th through 12th grades. They are the successors of today's business leaders. The problem is, approximately 30% of those students will drop out or fail to graduate on schedule. About 50% of minorities are dropping out. This gives the rest of the developed world a huge advantage over the United States in the upcoming economic wars.

If this problem isn't fixed fast, the United States will lose the next worldwide, economic, job-based war because its players can't read, write, or think as well as their competitors in a game for keeps — their talent doesn't get maximized. Even more deadly, Gallup suspects that those students' spirits and hope are being irreparably broken.

Educational researchers in the United States are quick to admit that the best science and efforts are nowhere near finding a solution to this problem. The Bill & Melinda Gates Foundation put together the best education scientists in the country, plus $2 billion, to allow some masters of the universe to experiment with several thousand K-12 schools to reduce the dropout rate. No success. The government put $4.35 billion into the Race to the Top fund, with no improvement yet in learning. Only 17% of charter schools outperform regular public schools. Great American institutions are trying every day to fix this problem, to see some improvement. So far, all have failed. Sure, there are a brilliant few who have performed magic at a school here or there, but their solutions have not proven to be scalable.

Does America need more rigorous national programs like No Child Left Behind that focus on grade improvement? Or possibly more money for teachers or a totally new merit system? Will Race to the Top become just another failed national program because nobody embraces it locally? Should Americans blame it on the teachers' unions protecting lousy teachers, or should they blame it on broken families and lousy parenting? Does the U.S. need a whole new system that builds better charter schools? America bounces around among all these solutions. None seem to work.

Some Americans might believe that government has to spend more money on education. Many leaders agree that this is the silver bullet. But Gallup continues to find, as we have for more than 75 years, that lots of money is rarely the solution to big problems. Sometimes, in fact, the bigger the problem, the less expensive the solution. What's expensive is trying to fix *after-the-fact* outcomes rather than creating strategies that get at the behaviors and cause.

This is leadership at its worst.

BEHAVIORAL ECONOMICS FOR PUBLIC SCHOOLS

Watching current trends, 43% of black males drop out of high school, and of that percentage, more than half eventually go to prison. These statistics and subsequent formulas help local leaders know how many prisons they need to build, but they don't tell them a thing about how to turn kids into economic engines.

What reverses this? Knowing what causes the dropout moment before it happens and the strategies to prevent it. This actually isn't that hard: Gallup has found that kids drop out of school *when they lose hope to graduate.* That's it. Not because they're lured into gangs or have to flip burgers to support their family.

The reason they lose hope of graduating is because they don't feel excited about what's next in their lives. The moment they feel that despair about what is ahead, they start psychologically dropping out. Having no vision or excitement for the future is the *cause* of dropping out of school. Students need to be rescued at or before the moment they lose hope in the future. And when they aren't caught in time, they don't just drop out of school, they drop out of life.

This can be fixed if America aims its strategies at the *cause* versus the *effects* of hopelessness. Therefore, leadership strategy must, first and foremost, be built on hope rather than on grades and attendance, because loss of hope precedes bad grades and truancy. Gallup scientists have learned that hope predicts academic success and graduation better than grades or test scores do.

Increasing hope isn't easy, but it can be done. And it has to be done locally, on a citywide basis rather than on a national one. Only a local focus has a chance.

This is what leaders have to do:

1. *Focus all local groups on student engagement, or the confidence to graduate.* I know this sounds too simple, but this is the very core of where Gallup scientists found student hope. That's the exact state of mind where the solution lies. Gallup's education research, as well as most other contributing data, states that the most important factor in student engagement is the teacher. Kids are affected by their families and communities, but the key to confidence is the teacher.

   Parents, teachers, and mentors would be wise to consider managing a student's confidence and hope as much as or more than the mechanics of division and multiplication. And the prize for a student is not graduating but rather a *job* — even better, an exciting career. Leaders need to consider that the system is putting all its resources into failed transactions rather than prevention.

There is a housekeeper in my apartment building named Mary. I met her 9-year-old son, AJ, one morning. He looked me right in the eye, and the first thing he said was, "Where do you work?" I told him, "Gallup." He asked what I do at Gallup, and I told him that we ask people questions, write down their answers, and then report what we learn. He thought that sounded like a great job and said, "Could I work there?"

I told him he would have to go through an interview first. So he came over one day and sat in my office, and I interviewed him while his mom waited downstairs. AJ was very well-prepared. He had gone on the Internet and learned about me and our founder, Dr. George Gallup. It was very impressive.

He and I then went around to Gallup associate offices and asked people what they did and how they earned a living at Gallup. He was really turned on by the thought of becoming a senior analyst. AJ's best subject is math.

AJ was impressed by Gallup, and Gallup was impressed by him. So I told him that he passed the interview and he was hired and that we expected him to come to work when he graduates, but he could work summers until then. I gave him a Gallup T-shirt and a hat.

He asked how to better prepare. I told him to always get top grades in math and be the leader of his favorite groups. AJ gets straight A's in math and is captain of his soccer team — near perfect prep for becoming a Gallup senior analyst.

AJ emails me with his progress at school. But he also emails me about numerous other jobs he might be interested in. He is careful not to hurt my feelings, but he has wondered about how much acting pays, how much becoming a doctor pays; he wondered about starting his own company. I told him he could start his own company and I would help him, but he should come to work at Gallup for at least a few years first.

AJ and I do not have a "grades" relationship. We have a "job" relationship. If he stays on his current path, there is no question that AJ will make a significant to downright famous contribution to the American workforce.

2. *Use Gallup's pro bono Student Poll as the core behavioral economic metric.* Administer it every spring and fall in every school in your city with every student. Gallup's Internet-based software is set up like a census, so you need to get

every student from 5th to 12th grade involved. The software surveys the kids and records their current state of mind. This will give your schools and city leaders their first ongoing behavioral economic metric — the first data they have ever had to build strategies before it is too late. Once a student's hope candle is blown out, it is nearly impossible to relight.

Gallup Student Poll Items:

1. Please imagine a ladder with steps numbered from zero at the bottom to ten at the top. The top of the ladder represents the best possible life for you and the bottom of the ladder represents the worst possible life for you. On which step of the ladder would you say you personally feel you stand at this time? On which step do you think you will stand about five years from now?

2. I know I will graduate from high school.

3. There is an adult in my life who cares about my future.

4. I can think of many ways to get good grades.

5. I energetically pursue my goals.

6. I can find lots of ways around any problem.

7. I know I will find a good job after I graduate.

8. I have a best friend at school.

9. I feel safe in this school.

10. My teachers make me feel my schoolwork is important.

11. At this school, I have the opportunity to do what I do best every day.

12. In the last seven days, I have received recognition or praise for doing good schoolwork.

13. My school is committed to building the strengths of each student.

14. In the last month, I volunteered my time to help others.

15. Were you treated with respect all day yesterday?

16. Did you smile or laugh a lot yesterday?

17. Did you learn or do something interesting yesterday?

18. Did you have enough energy to get things done yesterday?

19. Do you have health problems that keep you from doing any of the things other people your age normally can do?

20. If you are in trouble, do you have family or friends you can count on to help whenever you need them?

3. *Reduce by half the number of students with no hope of graduating.* When you and your leadership community halve this number, you will have fixed the dropout rate in your city or community because you put it on the road to correction.

4. *Involve all the local social-based organizations.* Have a big kickoff meeting. Call Operation HOPE in Atlanta, founded by John Bryant, and America's Promise Alliance in Washington, the group Colin Powell founded to provide a kind of air traffic control for almost all American youth programs — The Y, National 4-H Council, Girl Scouts of the USA, Junior Achievement, and so on. The kickoff meeting should have two agenda items: How can each of you have an impact on student confidence, and how can you align all these powerful forces to double it?

5. *Double student hope.* How? The groups attending your kickoff meeting will know. They have always had great people with super-powerful mission and purpose, and they will have far more answers than anybody else. As a group, they'll know every kid in town. They'll be student mentors, and they will be able to find others who can be. Every youth needs a mentor.

This will work.

If you take nothing else from this chapter, take these findings:

1. There are no national solutions to the debilitating dropout problem, and America can't buy its way out of it. All breakthroughs are local. Until all of the leaders in your city say, "I would rather die than lose my city's future" — which will happen if you don't fix this — and then they themselves take 100% responsibility for the solution, this problem will remain America's Achilles' heel. It really comes down to quality teachers and mentors for every child.

2. This is not a *public schools* problem. This needs to be burned deeply into your neurons. It is a *whole city* problem. Fixing the schools is about taking your whole city to war against the dropout problem — one student at a time, one school at a time, one city at a time.

3. Student graduation is one of the most definitive predictors of your city's future innovation, entrepreneurship, and subsequent job and GDP growth. If your city doesn't fix graduation rates and youth economic energy *now*, jobs that are perfect for it will move to Shanghai, Beijing, Santiago, Mumbai, Delhi, Seoul, Dublin, Sao Paulo, Mexico City, and Singapore.

4. If you were to ask me, from all of Gallup's data and research on entrepreneurship, what will most likely tell you if you

are winning or losing your city, my answer would be, "5th to 12th graders' image of and relationship to free enterprise and entrepreneurship." The better the image, the more likely your city will win. If your city doesn't have growing economic energy in your 5th through 12th graders, you will experience neither job creation nor city GDP growth.

Specifically, local leaders can use these key metrics to monitor 5th through 12th graders' potential for entrepreneurship and free enterprise:

1. I plan to start my own business.

2. I will invent something that changes the world.

3. My mind never stops.

4. I never give up.

5. I am not afraid to take risks even if I might fail.

6. I want to be my own boss.

7. The more education, the more money I will make.

8. My school teaches me about money and banking.

9. My school offers classes in how to start and run a business.

10. Do you have a bank or credit union account with money in it?

11. Are you currently interning with a local business?

12. Have either of your parents or guardians ever started a business?

13. Do you run your own business now?

14. How many hours did you work at any paying job last week?

These items are on the Gallup-HOPE Index. They measure your students' financial literacy and attitudes toward entrepreneurship and innovation, which in turn predict future economic energy in your city.

Cities need results from this survey from each school, but the most telling behavioral economic metric to watch is the direction and speed, the trends, of these markers. So, if the image of free enterprise and entrepreneurship is going up among your youth, you will experience job creation. If it is trending down, may God be with you.

Chapter Eleven

FIX HEALTHCARE OR DESTROY JOB CREATION

America's dropout rate is a disgrace and a disaster in the making. But it can be fixed with the tools on hand and caring, determined leaders.

There is, however, another looming problem hanging over America's job and GDP growth. And if it's not addressed, it will bankrupt the country and render the dropout rate and everything else I've discussed in this book irrelevant.

That problem is healthcare.

It is impossible for the U.S. to win the race for new good jobs while the country continues its failed strategies for healthcare. Astronomical healthcare costs end America's race to re-win the future. The United States has to fix this or it shuts off the energy switch to entrepreneurship and innovation. If this happens, everything else ceases to matter.

Healthcare costs are America's biggest current fiscal drain. I don't think any economist, left or right, would dispute this. So much money has been put into keeping sick people from getting sicker that virtually all other American institutions have been weakened. Healthcare is sucking the good money from a once-magnificent economic engine more than any leader has clearly articulated. The focus has been primarily on "who is without" and "who pays for what," not on actually lowering healthcare costs.

And here's a scary fact: Absolutely no institution or group in America has made any progress solving this. None. Zero. Everyone has tried, and everyone has failed. Congress has passed legislation on healthcare regarding *how it is paid for* not *how to lower costs*. So, regardless of what you read, see, and hear, total healthcare costs will continue to grow at staggering rates.

The current administration and Congress are working on how to *fund* the problem, not how to *solve* it. And few American leaders have the courage to solve it because the short-term and long-term pain of significantly reducing the costs of their constituencies' healthcare would be of historic magnitude. Leaders on both sides of the aisle probably have the intellectual strength to solve it, but not the courage.

Yet, because U.S. healthcare bills have reached such unimaginable amounts, it has to increase taxes not just on the rich, but on everyone and on all small, medium, and large businesses. America has reached the point where healthcare costs are suffocating everything at a time when the country simply can't afford it. The U.S. is spending too much of its resources on sickness instead of on winning new customers. The good money is going to the wrong place: preventable illness rather than sustainable job creation.

Furthermore, healthcare costs and their consequent taxes on small and medium-sized businesses sap confidence to reach out and grow. Huge healthcare costs undermine the all-important confidence of small and medium-sized businesses and ultimately cost jobs.

Cynics, and maybe rightly so, say that General Motors is a healthcare provider that gets its funding by making and selling cars. The company spent about $5.2 billion on healthcare in 2004, after all, which is a lot more than they spend on steel. It is not too hard to argue that the whole country survives just to make products and services to pay for its out-of-control healthcare costs. The costs have become that big.

Remember, the U.S. government doesn't "have money." The U.S. government allocates and spends money it collects from taxes. Unfortunately, it does print and borrow money from competitors like China. But that is a different problem, as is the fact that the government spends much more than it collects in revenues. But each new fiscal year, the government starts with nothing. No cash flow until taxes start coming in.

The country's decades-long supercharged economic run funded a huge U.S. government buildup of entitlements because it could — because a GDP jump to about $15 trillion over the last 30 years brought a super-rich tax base. Now, the enormous cash flow that the government and all its highly entitled citizens used to enjoy is being wiped out by healthcare costs. That's why healthcare is such a serious problem.

Healthcare is the United States' biggest most immediate fiscal budget problem, and there are no solutions so far because U.S. leaders dig in the wrong place. Here is what you as a leader need to know about the healthcare crisis to fix it in your city:

1. The recent healthcare reform bill is not a "healthcare bill." It is an insurance bill. It is a bill concerning coverage and payment. Nothing in it regards solutions to why America faces unaffordable costs or how to prevent health problems. It is a bill that changes how the money moves around. It is a bill about who gets healthcare and who pays for it.

2. The next big leadership breakthroughs in healthcare will be discovered within the sciences of behavioral economics, not medical laboratories. They definitely won't come from complex monetary policies that assign blame to everyone but the unfit American. The big fixes will be found in behavioral economics because the only way out of this is to focus on and encourage Americans to make different eating, smoking,

exercise, and lifestyle choices — prevention, in other words. Remember the Japanese official who said Americans had become fat and lazy? Gallup economics concludes that unless many of the 300 million U.S. citizens change their relationship to their lifestyle, especially the food they eat, there is no way to stop healthcare costs from spiraling out of control.

3. The Gallup-Healthways Well-Being Index, which is the largest study on wellbeing ever, concluded that obese and overweight people have less physical and psychological energy than the fit, that people who don't get enough sleep have less energy, and that people who worry about their finances have higher levels of stress. This leads to unaffordable healthcare costs as well as a sluggish American workforce. Ultimately, unfit people cost American taxpayers trillions of dollars that could have been spent on creating more jobs.

4. The only fix lies within the highly aligned strategies of cities and companies to improve health and wellbeing, especially focusing on reducing obesity as successfully as they did with cigarette smoking.

Unless it is fixed, the healthcare mess will break the U.S. economy and hand the future of capitalism and the best jobs to China, India, and others. I am not overstating this. Healthcare costs alone will break the country because the numbers are so big. America can't buy its way out of this problem like it has with so many others.

Before I answer how behavioral economics-based leadership could solve this catastrophic problem for the United States and your city, let's review the size and scope of this incoming meteorite of unsustainable costs.

SIZE OF THE PROBLEM

1. The United States spent $2,500,000,000,000 on healthcare in 2009 — two and a half trillion dollars. Nearly half of this comes from Medicare and Medicaid (taxes). And the other half is private insurance and out-of-pocket spending.

2. This is the biggest price tag for anything in America. War in Iraq and Afghanistan run about $200 billion per year. The healthcare bill per year is 10 times bigger than the annual war bill. Almost no one I talk to knows this. Sometimes I hear caring Americans say, "Well if we weren't fighting these wars, we could afford healthcare for everyone." Wrong. Eliminating what America is paying to fight wars wouldn't be nearly enough to solve the healthcare mess.

3. The healthcare bill for 300 million Americans is $2.5 trillion per year. The entire economy of India, with a population of 1 billion people, is right under $1.5 trillion — not their

healthcare bill, their whole GDP. Russia's whole GDP is also right under $1.5 trillion — not their healthcare bill, their whole economy.

4. America averages about $8,000 per year per person for healthcare. When diagnosed with Type 2 diabetes or high blood pressure, for example, some Americans take pills and continue an unhealthy lifestyle rather than simply eating less and exercising more. Obese citizens with failing knee and hip joints will undergo replacement surgeries rather than simply lose weight, which often fixes the problem. These are simple examples of how misguided choices are killing a once great nation. Strong, productive societies in countries like England, Germany, Canada, and France pay less than half that per citizen. Their people live longer than Americans do, and they rate the quality of their healthcare as high as U.S. citizens rate their own.

5. Finally, the problem is getting worse fast because healthcare costs, according to the U.S. government's own figures, will grow at just over 6% per year for the next 10 years. So the total amount that America can't afford now of $2.5 trillion is growing significantly faster than the economy and will hit $4.5 trillion within 10 years. If you take the total amount of increase over the current $2.5 trillion that America already can't afford and total the sum of the annual increases over the full 10 years, that 10-year summed increase is nearly $10

trillion. So the United States has to come up with about $10 trillion more than it already doesn't have over the next 10 years. This amount of money will not magically appear. You might think the U.S. can borrow it from China, but they're not going to loan anyone $10 trillion. And nobody, including China, has that much cash lying around. The United States is running massive deficits now. This $10 trillion makes the whole nation-ruining deficit insurmountable, unless it is stopped in its tracks.

So that is the size and scope of the problem. Americans grossly overuse doctors, pills, and all medical services and actually die younger than do the British, French, Canadians, and Germans.

Very few U.S. leaders know these basic facts.

One more math run: The whole subprime mess — caused by desperate bankers trying to hit badly needed short-term numbers when nothing else was shaking, caffeinated by 20 years of government leaders slowly and then suddenly loosening borrowing regulations; plus the negligent ratings of oversight agencies; as well as the 10 million people who signed up for loans they never should have accepted (a key factor that isn't discussed much) — cost the country only about $3 trillion. *Only* $3 trillion. And it brought America and much of the world to its knees. It was worse than any economic, social, or international crisis since the Great Depression, and still, nobody knows for sure where it will end.

Yet the healthcare problem is more than three times worse. The subprime debacle was a 3-trillion-story tsunami, and the next one coming is a 10-trillion-story tsunami. Too few leaders in business and government know this.

PREVENTION

Yet the solutions to this overwhelming problem are actually staring everyone right in the face.

The Centers for Disease Control and Prevention (CDC) reports that more than 75% of the total $2.5 trillion healthcare spending is on people with chronic, and in most cases preventable, conditions such as diabetes, heart disease, and obesity. If Americans just took newfound individual responsibility for their own health, lifestyle, and wellbeing, the looming healthcare disaster could be miraculously fixed.

Researchers at Rutgers University reported that "Last-year-of-life expenses constituted 22% of all medical, 26% of Medicare, 18% of all non-Medicare expenditures, and 25% of Medicaid expenditures."

Thomson Reuters did a massive study and put the cost of total healthcare waste at $600 to $850 billion and said figuring that "one-third of annual healthcare expenditures as waste is reasonable and maybe even conservative." One-third of what the U.S. spends on healthcare falls off the table.

Next time you hear how well the American healthcare system is run, remember this. It is hard to believe. Experts estimate that as many as 98,000 people are killed in hospitals each year because of medical mistakes. Another 1,000,000+ are injured from mistakes that they live through.

A hospital is, honest to God, a more dangerous place to be than Iraq or Afghanistan. Over the last eight years, about 6,000 American soldiers have been killed while fighting in Iraq and Afghanistan. During the same time, nearly 800,000 American patients have been killed by healthcare mistakes — and about 8,000,000 injured. War fatalities are so small compared to what is happening in hospitals and healthcare facilities. And of course, patients aren't dying for their country.

Unless drastically changed, healthcare costs will be the thing that wipes America out. And those costs bring the whole world economy down with them because the United States remains the whole world's golden goose — now a very obese and sick golden goose.

The fact is that America needs healthcare solutions that cut the costs in half, not that move the payers around. The right number for U.S. national healthcare is $1,250,000,000,000 per year — exactly half what it is today. Same with your city: Healthcare costs in your city are exactly two times what they should and can be. I will admit that cutting these costs in half is pretty far away. Actually, the problem cities and organizations have to varying degrees is just dealing with current runaway increases. The costs that nobody can afford are growing and getting worse at a clip of about 6% a year. If you're an American, you can watch your world coming apart within this 6%. It upsets everything because it is so big, and it's growing.

CITY PROBLEM, CITY SOLUTIONS

Where can leaders start to tackle this immense problem? As with education, not nationally, but in cities, where extreme differences in healthcare costs and outcomes now exist. And once again, behavioral economics offers the keys to a lasting solution.

To grossly oversimplify, classical economics says change the money. Behavioral economics says change the behavior because behavior happens before the money. Everything Washington is doing now deals with the accounting. A classical economist's view is that if America can get a new scheme for the payments, it can solve this. A behavioral economic view is that if America can get the masses to make different decisions about their lifestyles, then the country can solve this.

The classical economic view doesn't solve anything; it just pays for growing debt in slightly different ways. Moving the money around might change incentives and create subsequent tiny gains, but that barely affects the behavior, which is where all the big money is. *Very* big money.

Right now, U.S. citizens are choosing to spend trillions on extending their lives six months. What your congressperson will never tell you is that Americans no longer have an unlimited amount of money to keep the dying alive a little longer. It's sad and devastatingly personal, but the fact is, America doesn't have the tax base to do it. Nevertheless, that's where a lot of the U.S. healthcare dollars go. For obvious reasons, it's a problem your elected officials are reluctant to address or even approach. Somehow people have to adjust their relationship to dying or face issues of far bigger human magnitude.

Add to that what obesity is costing. The CDC reports that 70% of the $2.5 trillion America spends on healthcare goes toward preventable diseases. And a leading cause of preventable diseases is obesity, which has been associated with increased risk for Type 2 diabetes and other chronic conditions, which in turn is the catalyst for everything that goes wrong. The CDC concludes that more than two-thirds of American adults, aged 20 and older, are simply too fat. Approximately one-third of Americans are a healthy weight, one-third are overweight, and one-third are obese. This is a significant contributor to roughly 70% of the $2.5 trillion annual healthcare expense.

Obviously, if all Americans were fit, the healthcare problem — the cost and the human toll — would miraculously be fixed. Having fit Americans might magically fix everything because, besides the cost savings, fit people are more productive than obese people.

Every year, the U.S. loses billions in health costs and productivity to obesity. Fit people create more customers and new jobs.

The bottom line is that the big solutions lie within getting people to eat differently and changing their relationship to death.

I know this is a tall order, and it makes things more difficult for leaders, but they need to step up. Unless the elephant in the room is addressed, the United States will fail to experience job growth — all of the good money will go to enabling the poor health habits of the American people.

Moving the money around, as Washington is doing now, not only fails to solve the problem, it enables the citizenry to keep making bad choices and maintaining unhealthy lifestyles. It suggests that there are no real consequences because a doctor is always available with a prescription and a scalpel, and someone else will pay for all of it. This method puts the blame in the wrong place, which feeds the problem and allows it to get worse. And the message from Washington seems to be that it is one's right as an American to be unfit.

The U.S. needs big money and great medicine for people, especially children, with all kinds of conditions that modern medicine can miraculously heal. But the money won't be there if it's all spent on keeping Uncle Louie alive for another three months. Somebody has to tell Uncle Louie it's time to cross to the other side and go join his friends, not run doctor to doctor, accepting one low-probability procedure after another.

BEHAVIORAL ECONOMICS — WHAT WORKED

America can accomplish essential changes in behavior. Look what happened to another American "right": smoking. When I was a kid, virtually everyone smoked. People smoked in church, stores, restaurants, buses, airplanes — my doctor smoked while he examined me. In college, my English class would fill the room with smoke. Now, the smoking rate has been cut in half and continues to decline.

Years ago, Gallup research teams were part of a breakthrough that concluded that peer pressure for smokers, especially young people, was by far the biggest factor in the decision to smoke or not to smoke — not because it's lethal. Because the consequences aren't immediate, calling smoking fatally dangerous wasn't sufficiently persuasive to change kids' habits. It didn't create enough fear. It didn't scare them enough to change their behavior. Young people often believe they are immortal, so they judge the danger of lighting a cigarette using this test: "Will this one cigarette kill me?" Most likely the answer to that question for them is *no.* That one cigarette won't cause sickness and cancer, so they smoke it.

Then they ask, "Will this next one kill me?" And the answer to that question too is most likely for them *no*, not that second cigarette either. But what will make you sick and likely kill you is the long-term pattern of smoking. But kids don't make decisions based on long-term patterns. The concept that a systematic pattern of smoking will kill you doesn't create enough fear or discomfort for them to stop, so they smoke the next cigarette.

When young people learned that their smoking affected their personal *brand*, that it created a negative image — one of lower intelligence and income and other uncomplimentary attributes — they chose not to light up. Changing the decision-making tree for young people based on immediate damage to their personal brand versus their personal health changed their smoking behaviors. It worked; they quit.

What made an enormous difference in youth smoking behaviors was changing the image and then creating new policies about that image that supported the message. The primary trigger for reducing smoking among adults was city ordinances against smoking in restaurants and public places of all kinds. The workplace came next. Also helping are some courts allowing companies to fire employees for smoking anywhere, on or off the job, which also sent a very strong message. Banning TV ads that suggest smoking is cool helped too.

But here's the big thing: 30 years ago, if I had said that Americans would no longer have a right to smoke — that no one could smoke anywhere in the city of Minneapolis, New York, Omaha, or Topeka except outside on the curb — there wouldn't have been a person in the world who would have believed me. If I had said that the percentage of people who smoke, including youth, would suddenly be cut in half, nobody would have believed it.

What made all that come to pass was creating a necessary fear about the short-term discomforts of bad image versus the long-term discomfort of cancer and dying. What worked was a change in the premise of what would alter people's decision-making process, their state of mind, when they decided not to light up.

Behavioral economics changed the smoking problem. One could even argue that the smoking problem is fixed because the mathematical trend is moving toward zero. This is as clear of an example of how leaders can use behavioral economics to solve big problems as there is.

In fact, there are other examples of this. Remember littering? Fifty years ago, when my dad and I would go fishing, we would throw our lunch sacks out the car window. If you were standing on the road and saw us do that, you would have thought nothing about it at all — there was no negative concept of littering.

All that changed decades ago. In 1982, litter on Texas highways had been growing at an average rate of 17% each year. The Texas Highway Commission was discussing increasing the budget to keep up with this increase in litter because that was the national trend and the only solution anyone could come up with. After hearing the request for a 17% increase in state funding for the antilitter program, the chairman asked if rather than spending more of taxpayers' money on picking up litter, why didn't they persuade Texans *not to litter?*

To me, that is a legitimate Nobel Prize moment. The resulting cause-based behavioral economics campaign went on to forever change the perception of littering in Texas. "Don't Mess with Texas" became one of the most recognized slogans in America. And Texas reduced litter by 70% in five years by tapping into Texans' fierce pride in their state, creating a powerful initiative that cleaned up the state's highways and cut its budgets. A seemingly intractable American bad habit was fixed by dealing with the cause rather than spending more on the effect.

Back to healthcare. One has to wonder if the root cause of the healthcare problem is just bad leadership. America seems to be simply agreeing to pay for healthcare for people who have made themselves sick. It's paying some portion of $2.5 trillion to "pick up the litter" rather than creating more powerful messages about why people should stop.

Indeed, the opposite is happening. People are getting the message that they should go ahead and eat the chips and develop lifelong health problems. But if you care about the future of the country, being unfit matters a lot. So leaders need to send a new message using the image-based, behavioral economic solution that worked with smoking.

Unfit should mean something worse than it currently does. Unfit should mean "intervention required." Unfit should mean less employable because unfit is a cause of lower energy. Unfit should mean unfit for leadership positions, just like smoking does. You might notice that few elected officials, top military generals, favorite CEOs and chairmen, the influential talking heads, or any famous or highly admired leader of any sort are obese or smoke. Navy SEALs can't choose to be fat. The United States military has a crude, never-written euphemism for obese leaders who get passed over. They refer to the unfit in whispers as "lacking parade presence."

That's not all that the unfit lack, according to Gallup's research.

BEHAVIORAL ECONOMICS OF WELLBEING

The United States needs critical leadership positions to be held by the fittest people, in every sense, as they will require their constituencies to be fit as well. Gallup has taken one of its deepest dives into the behavioral economics of healthcare and sickness and has discovered five key elements of wellbeing. If leaders create behavioral-based strategies and policies to improve these five elements, all good things will follow for their constituencies.

Career Wellbeing: how you occupy your time or simply liking what you do every day.

Social Wellbeing: having strong relationships and love in your life.

Financial Wellbeing: effectively managing your economic life.

Physical Wellbeing: having good health and enough energy to get things done on a daily basis.

Community Wellbeing: the sense of engagement you have with the area where you live.

These elements represent broad categories that are essential to most people. The United States can't create the best jobs until these five key behavioral economic indicators become the new demands of all leadership — and until they are subsequently woven into the fabric of the culture. If all American leaders in every walk of life, from companies to playgrounds, improved these wellbeing states of mind among their constituencies, they would fix the U.S. healthcare problem. And the jobs problem. And the entrepreneur problem. And everything else.

If you knew that obesity was what kept you from getting hired or promoted, getting dated or befriended, getting included or respected at all, that alone would fix the healthcare problem. The math that would fix the healthcare problem and save the U.S. economic engine is pretty easy: If twice as many Americans were fit, problem solved. And it goes back to leading the free world because the money and energy implications are that enormous.

If one-third of overweight Americans became fit, so that two-thirds were healthy, problem solved. Fixing obesity would nearly eradicate Type 2 diabetes. And fixing obesity would free up significantly more money than the current tax proposals would dredge out of American pockets. There is no single act of leadership that has bigger money implications than simply doubling the number of fit Americans.

Or look at it this way: Significantly reducing the percentage of obese Americans would save multiple times more taxpayer money than pulling all U.S. troops out of both Iraq and Afghanistan.

The American people are confused about these numbers because they are so big and complex. Americans have to be led better. Then, not only would the country *not* need to raise taxes on every household and business or print more "pretend" new money at the U.S. Treasury and then generate more pretend jobs with pretend value, as it's doing now — but America could suddenly create budget surpluses, not to mention more productive, more energetic, high-producing citizens who are more inspired to create more entrepreneurial energy. The numbers are that large.

There are no solutions to the healthcare problem where American leaders are currently digging. Moving the money around isn't a solution. Solutions lie within changing behavior.

A nation in which two-thirds of its constituents are obese or in poor health — or soon will be because of their weight, lack of exercise, addiction to cigarettes, bad diets, and general low wellbeing — will never win the upcoming fight against foreign economic competitors. Workers won't be fit enough to win.

Healthcare costs are diverting virtually all the money Americans ought to be spending on innovation, entrepreneurship, and consequently job creation. Healthcare costs are overwhelming small, medium, and large businesses. Most specifically, healthcare costs create significant uncertainty as the government wrestles with how to pay the bills and pass them on to businesses — mostly small and medium-sized businesses.

So until these unaffordable costs are reversed, until Americans greatly improve their health behaviors, the country is at too much of a competitive disadvantage to win the global war for good jobs.

Chapter Twelve

GLOBAL WELLBEING

Let's broaden the scope now to global wellbeing and global behavioral economics. America needs all countries to do well if for no other reason than the business partnerships they have with America. The best and most sustainable relationship for the United States to have with another country is a business relationship — not a political relationship, not an aid relationship, not a defense relationship, but a business relationship. And America has to lead the world in great business relationships based on exchanging goods because human development, peace, and all good things flow from there. Foremost among them is simple wellbeing.

WELLBEING DEFINED

Wellbeing is the mathematical description of the emotional and psychological state of your city, your nation, your constituency, and your followers. It is the mathematical description of whether they're suffering, struggling, or thriving; their hope; their physical health;

whether they have pain in their body or sickness; whether they get a good night's sleep; and whether they get worried, stressed, sad, lonely, angry, or depressed. It's whether they had a good day and a good year — a good life.

Almost no one knows or understands this: *Gross national wellbeing (GNW) occurs before GDP* in cities and countries. GNW, or the lack of it, occurs before revolutions and before significant political change. This means that virtually all world leaders and heads of states and cities are managing most of the wrong things. They are looking through the rearview mirror in an attempt to see the road ahead. Consequently, they are managing their countries and cities after the fact. Because GDP follows GNW, leaders need to understand the way wellbeing works, the impact it has on constituencies, and most importantly, how to change it.

At the end of each day, most people can say if it has been a good day. In fact, they can probably say if it has been a good week, month, year, or lifetime. Now, if you ask people about their day in a little more detail — "Did you get enough to eat?" or "Did you spend any time with friends?" — and collect and measure the answers, as Gallup does, you'll get a consistent, reliable measure of wellbeing.

In fact, Gallup has been asking wellbeing questions in more than 150 countries for the past six years. The responses have been subjected to a university math department-worth of statistical analysis so that a lot of complex numbers can be described simply as a "ladder of life."

Building on the Cantril Self-Anchoring Striving Scale, Gallup measures life satisfaction by asking respondents to rate their lives on a ladder scale, with steps numbered from 0 to 10. So one of the best measures of wellbeing for anyone on Earth is these questions:

Please imagine a ladder with steps numbered from 0 at the bottom to 10 at the top. The top of the ladder represents the best possible life for you and the bottom of the ladder represents the worst possible life for you.

On which step of the ladder would you say you personally feel you stand at this time?

Just your best guess, on which step do you think you will stand in the future, say about five years from now?

Based on how respondents rate their current and future lives, Gallup scientists categorize them as "thriving," "struggling," or "suffering." Gallup has found that, worldwide, those who have "good jobs" — those who are employed by an employer and work for that employer for at least 30 hours per week — are most likely to be thriving. Those who are employed part time and those who are unemployed are less likely to be thriving. The self-employed lag behind and are the least likely to be thriving.

Clearly, work status makes a difference in how people rate their lives.

Furthermore, Gallup has found that the answers to wellbeing questions are highly correlated with other external ratings taken separately and independently. For instance, Gallup knows that those living in wealthier countries tend to have higher subjective wellbeing than those living in poor countries. While money doesn't guarantee happiness, living in a wealthy country certainly increases your odds of having a good life.

Angus Deaton, one of the world's foremost economists, looked into the relationship between wellbeing and measures of health, such as life expectancy and prevalence of HIV, and concluded that the relationship between health and wellbeing is based on the *expectation* of health and not actual health status.

That's an interesting and important point. Expectations are everything. You might hate being sick, but you'll hate it a lot less if you think you'll be cured soon. For that reason, leaders need to watch the direction that GNW is trending. Great GNW that's heading downward is worse for a city than poor GNW that's getting a little better every year.

Gallup has also found that as thriving decreases and suffering increases in a country or region, the country or region becomes more unstable. This critical behavioral metric will become more and more important to countries and cities as they are forced to make drastic cuts in government jobs as well as other government entitlements. They will need to keep a close eye on the growing percentage of people who are suffering because that number is an indicator of potential extreme citizen discomfort and unrest — even chaos. On average, about two countries per year descend into revolution; Gallup economics has found that one of the key conditions necessary for revolution is whether more and more citizens are suffering.

And, importantly, Gallup's research indicates that having a good job is probably essential to having a sense of higher wellbeing. In fact, as the Gallup Path to Global Wellbeing shows, three of the eight necessary steps to thriving global wellbeing involve jobs.

GALLUP PATH TO GLOBAL WELLBEING

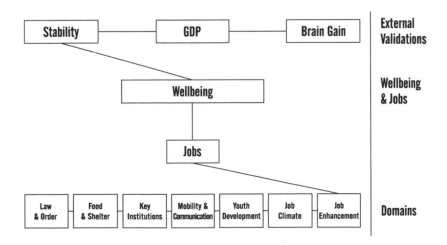

THE FIRST STEPS

Before a city or a country can obtain almighty job creation and then job growth, it has to perform well on the eight steps of wellbeing — in order — or the remaining linkages will not occur. That is one of the major breakthroughs of the Gallup Path to Global Wellbeing: *The hierarchy of needs has an order, and it must be kept.* These steps on the path make individual wellbeing possible, without which national wellbeing is very hard to achieve.

STEP 1: LAW AND ORDER

Absence of fear is the first of the new demands of world leadership. Gallup found that two behavioral economic questions apply to every neighborhood in the world, and they are the best indicators of residents' state of mind of fear:

- *Do you feel safe walking alone at night in the city or area where you live?*

- *In the city or area where you live, do you have confidence in the local police force?*

As these behavioral economic metrics improve, so does GNW, and then GDP.

These questions don't refer to crime. They refer to fear because fear sucks energy from potential economic activities. Safety is therefore absolutely critical. But *law and order* cannot be measured by crime statistics because those don't measure fear. They measure how many crimes were reported and how many bad guys were caught.

The traditional bureaucracy of data and the classical economics of crime run the risk of misrepresenting the facts. For instance, when more police officers are put on the beat, crime appears to go up. The more police on patrol, the more criminals are caught. Therefore, crime figures go up when police officers are added. That doesn't mean crime has gone up or that it will go down. Sometimes crime increases because the community fears the police as much as the bad guys, so they don't report the crimes. Law and order may appear to be improving when it is actually getting worse.

For that reason, the amount of fear a population feels is more telling. Gallup found that a person's level of fear is best measured by the answer to the question "Do you feel safe walking alone at night in the city or area where you live?" That accurately measures fear everywhere, for an impoverished mother in Ethiopia to a Parisian professor.

That said, women in sub-Saharan Africa say they don't feel safe walking just a hundred meters from their villages because they fear being raped or beaten. Thus, they can't walk to markets to buy or sell goods. When and if their fear is lifted, they'll increase Africa's GDP a little or a lot because they will be able to contribute their own local economic energy.

I live in Georgetown, an affluent neighborhood in Washington, D.C. Several years ago, we had a serious crime spree. People started going home directly after work and staying in. We didn't feel safe walking alone after dark. The community significantly decreased its spending on shopping and dining out. Our restaurants and shops lost a lot of their GDP until law and order was restored through an ambitious effort by local law enforcement. It wasn't until then that our GDP returned to normal because it wasn't until then that our fear subsided. The relationship of safety to GDP went back to normal.

Three or four decades ago, much of New York City was too dangerous to visit. Then, New York's leadership suddenly and rather miraculously locked it down — and the city's GDP increased, mostly by delivering law and order. The same thing happened in Bogota recently. City and national leadership cleaned up this once lethally dangerous city, and Bogota's restaurants and shops filled back up. GDP growth increased.

Places like Singapore or Luxembourg have little to gain from improving their residents' safety state of mind because their residents have little to no fear of physical harm as it is. Singapore and Abu Dhabi have maxed out safety, so they have to concentrate on different steps, where they have bigger problems.

STEP 2: FOOD AND SHELTER

Once people feel safe in their country, city, and neighborhood, their next most important state of wellbeing is adequate food and shelter. Sufficient food and shelter permit them to have enough energy to do the things other people their age can do. Being physically or mentally wiped out because of lack of food and shelter is a nonstarter.

Gallup uses two key questions to monitor this behavioral economic condition worldwide:

- *Have there been times in the past 12 months when you did not have enough money to buy food that you or your family needed?*

- *Have there been times in the past 12 months when you did not have enough money to provide adequate shelter or housing for you and your family?*

If the biggest demand of my day is getting food and/or finding decent shelter, then I am not in a position to add energy to the local economy as do other world residents. I am clearly out of the game.

Having enough food and adequate shelter are key behavioral metrics for leaders to track, not only because they occur before job and GDP growth on the Path, but also because without these basic requirements, the populace doesn't have the energy to solve its everyday problems.

STEP 3: KEY INSTITUTIONS

The billions of dollars spent on global institutions in countries and cities won't improve job creation and GDP until law and order and food and shelter are nailed down. Law and order comes first, before everything. Without it, nothing else is possible. Next in importance is food and shelter.

Institutions — particularly the availability of healthcare and educational institutions — are third most important. Part of this is more emotional than material, however, in that the questions also measure people's confidence in their leaders.

The questions Gallup uses are direct:

- *In the city or area where you live, are you satisfied or dissatisfied with the educational system or the schools?*

- *In the city or area where you live, are you satisfied or dissatisfied with the availability of quality healthcare?*

These two simple straightforward questions are associated with major wellbeing issues such as adult literacy rates and infant mortality.

STEP 4: MOBILITY AND COMMUNICATION

The mere existence of institutions is not enough. In Cuba, for example, citizens indicate high levels of satisfaction with healthcare and education, but not many people would consider Cuba a hotbed of new job creation. One of the reasons may be that Cubans seriously lack mobility.

The ability to simply move around is important for economies, especially as it applies to job development. Workers have to be able to go where the jobs are. Entrepreneurs have to go where the entrepreneurial energy is hot. Then, when the new businesses aren't new anymore, when they're stable and growing, they need to be able to expand. Meanwhile, mobility isn't just physical; mobility of thought and expression is important too.

Gallup uses these questions to monitor mobility and communication around the world:

- *In the city or area where you live, are you satisfied or dissatisfied with the public transportation systems?*

- *In the city or area where you live, are you satisfied or dissatisfied with the roads and highways?*

- *Does your home have a cellular phone?*

- *Does your home have access to the Internet?*

STEPS 5, 6, AND 7: YOUTH DEVELOPMENT, JOB CLIMATE, AND JOB ENHANCEMENT

To get and keep jobs, a city or country must be seen as job friendly and work ready. Obviously, people need a reason to think that, and they get that reason from entrepreneurs.

Entrepreneurs are the rainmakers. They're the ones creating jobs, customers, money, and the reason to believe a city offers all three. When enough strong entrepreneurs gather in a city and create formal jobs, they start a virtuous cycle. They provide the energy for the job creation machine, which provides the profits that pay taxes, which support the educational system, which develops the workers, who run the jobs machine, and on and on.

To determine whether that's happening, Gallup asks these questions:

Youth Development

- *Do you believe that children in this country are treated with respect and dignity, or not?*

- *Do most children in this country have the opportunity to learn and grow every day, or not?*

Job Climate

- *Thinking about the job situation in the city or area where you live today, would you say that it is now a good time or a bad time to find a job?*

- *In the city or area where you live, are you satisfied or dissatisfied with the availability of good job opportunities?*

Job Enhancement

- *Can people in this country get ahead by working hard, or not?*

- *Is the city or area where you live a good place or not a good place to live for entrepreneurs forming new businesses?*

When youth development, job climate, and job enhancement are considered healthy and growing, all good things follow.

A GOOD JOB

When those preconditions are met, a city or country has a good foundation for the creation of good jobs. But how does a leader know if the jobs are good jobs? Leaders should closely track three primary markers: *Do I have a good job? Is this a good city or country for a person like me to find a good job? Is this a good place for entrepreneurs?* When people can affirm all three, the city or country is on track for good GNW, and people can achieve the great global dream of having a good job.

Great GNW, however, can only result from enough great jobs. Having a great job means:

1. You have a good job — meaning you are employed full time for an employer and work at least 30 hours per week for this

employer — rather than a subsistence job that does little to raise you out of poverty or contribute to your country's formal economic output.

2. You know what is expected of you at work, and you have an inherent capacity to perform your tasks at work.

3. Your boss takes an interest in your success and development.

4. Your opinion counts at work.

5. You feel that your job has an important mission and purpose.

When these five elements are present in a job, people's life outcomes are different. Everything around them is different; it is better. The preconditions I previously outlined and the development of good jobs lead to positive wellbeing. Those citizens with good jobs, those with everyday steady income, and those who are truly engaged at work are at the top of the wellbeing ladder. This leads to positive GDP and to more stable, viable countries. It also leads to a key ingredient in long-term success: brain gain.

BRAIN GAIN

Leaders who have thriving constituencies — people who think their lives are good and will get better — are likelier to see brain gain in their cities. Gallup defines brain gain as reflecting a city's or country's ability to attract and retain talented people whose exceptional gifts and knowledge create new business and new jobs to help improve that city's or country's economy.

The challenge that leaders face now is how to trigger brain gain in their cities. Talent is an incredibly valuable commodity because it's at the core of entrepreneurship and innovation. It's the extreme differentiator of all mankind. And talent attracts more talent.

Consider the technology industry. If you are a technology inventor or entrepreneur, virtually everything you need — from a network of inventors and entrepreneurs to investors to super mentors — is in or near Silicon Valley. Think of it as the "Nashville Rule": If you have talent to produce country music, you'll have more opportunity to maximize that talent and be surrounded by great country musicians and record-company entrepreneurs in Nashville than generally anywhere else in the world.

And the Nashville Rule hinges on surprisingly few people. Much of the unexpected total Internet technology boom can be traced back to 1,000 people. Of these 1,000, more than half were Americans who had migrated from other countries. This is a critical piece of data. Of these 500 or so immigrants, many were from India. So if, say, 300 to 400 Indians hadn't moved to Silicon Valley — drawn in large part by Berkeley and Stanford — it is possible that the huge economic rise wouldn't have happened at all. Not here, and not in India — Bangalore and Mumbai don't have the fertile conditions for quick maximization of innovation or entrepreneurship that the greater San Francisco Valley has.

IMPLICATIONS FOR AMERICA

America can't win the coming jobs war without attracting the best talent and helping the talented become American citizens *fast*. The country can't lead the world economy without a disproportionate market share of the most talented people in the world.

The next big economic city empires will rise up where the most talented entrepreneurs migrate and stay. National policies on immigration of unusually gifted people to America need to be changed or the country will lose the next generation of jobs. America has to attract half, or a minimum of one-third, of these talented people if it is to win again.

Let me be very clear and say that again: America needs to attract one-third to one-half of the most unusually talented people in the world. This is the most powerful human resources strategy the country has. America has to do all the things I have previously mentioned to win, but attracting the most unusually talented people, especially the most talented entrepreneurs, will most likely create another sudden economic miracle.

QUALITY GDP GROWTH AND JOB CREATION

If you were to ask me, after reviewing everything Gallup scientists could find, including 75 years of survey research data, what role human nature and behavioral economics play in the phenomenon of job creation, I would say *wellbeing*. The elements of wellbeing are the frames of mind that occur before everything good or bad that happens in your country or city.

Gross national wellbeing is critical to GDP growth because job creation, entrepreneurship, and innovation aren't fueled by miserable or sick people. Miserable citizens don't create good jobs, and they aren't very good workers either. Any time you improve wellbeing, your city or country will get a little to a lot better; it will create a few or a lot more jobs.

The steps on the Gallup Path to Global Wellbeing are the markers of wellbeing; they are the very soul of your city and the hope of your country. Business and NGO leaders should incorporate these behavioral economic metrics into their global strategies. Leaders need to know that people are better off and more likely to have high job-related wellbeing and to be thriving when they are employed in good jobs.

The more residents with *good jobs* there are in a country or city, the better. All of these individuals' inventions and business models should make creating good jobs — by country and city — *their core mission*. The Gallup Path to Global Wellbeing is quite simply a global road map for the world's most needed aspects of wellbeing.

If every American organization included its impact on another country's society in its strategic plan for foreign partnerships, U.S. businesses could do more for global peace than the State Department, the World Bank, and the United Nations combined. And the country would win the best jobs. There is no conversation more respectful and desired anywhere in the world than one about customers, job creation, business partnerships, equity, and entrepreneurship.

Regardless of the goods it trades overseas — bridges, tunnels, tons of technology, education, food, and medicine — America will export more when it ties its products to these steps that improve the wellbeing of other countries. This should be the worldwide mission of every American business. By improving in the wellbeing step that is most related to its products and services, every business can improve the country's wellbeing. So U.S. businesses aren't just looking for deals anymore, they're exporting to improve their customers' gross national wellbeing.

There are unlimited amounts of money, revenue, profits, stock increase, jobs, and GDP growth connected to tying all corporate strategies to wellbeing steps on this path. But what too few recognize is that even elusive world peace is attainable when and if American businesses have winning partnerships virtually everywhere in the world.

Young people, old people, rich and poor, Russians, Ethiopians, Peruvians, Muslims, Hindus, Kurds, Christians, and all different races and cultures — whether you are an ad executive, an army general, a Peace Corps volunteer, or a missionary — the No. 1 topic in the world and for years to come is job creation and entrepreneurship. American strategies should tie everything to these gross national wellbeing path steps. These steps represent the next generation of human development and the next test of whether humankind can survive together.

CONCLUSION

From all Gallup's data, which have been gathered from asking the whole world questions on virtually everything, the most profound finding is this: The primary *will of the world* is no longer about peace or freedom or even democracy; it is not about having a family, and it is neither about God nor about owning a home or land. The will of the world is first and foremost to have a good job. Everything else comes after that. A good job is a social value. That is a huge sociological shift for humankind. It changes everything about how people lead countries, cities, and organizations.

Earlier, I mentioned that though biased toward America because I'm American and believe that America is an exceptional country and should lead the world, what I say in this book is true for every developed nation — and *good* for every nation, developed or not. The world gets better as its leading countries get better.

For America to lead the new will of the world, it will have to master 10 demands — 10 findings that are the most important of the literally trillions of combinations of data and opinions Gallup has studied:

1. The biggest problem facing the world is an inadequate supply of good jobs. Every leader in every institution and organization must consider this in every decision he or she makes every day. The great global dream is now focused on having a good job. If you are the best in the world at something other than creating strategies and policies aimed at the great global dream, your leadership now has less value. Job creation is the new currency of all world leaders. The new most important social value in the world no longer relates to human rights, the environment, abortion, religion, gay marriage, women's issues, or equality. The No. 1 social value in the world is *my job*.

2. Job creation can only be accomplished in cities. There is huge variation of local GDP and job creation outcomes by city. Cities can be influenced and changed more than whole countries. The federal government cannot create sustainable jobs, just short-term ones. Jobs are as local as politics. Cities are job power plants of human energy, which creates jobs through innovation and especially through entrepreneurship.

3. There are three key energy sources of job creation in America: the country's top 100 cities, its top 100 universities, and its 10,000 local tribal leaders. There are

many other moving parts of job creation, but these are the most dependable and manageable. They are the best strengths to leverage. They are America's supercollider for jobs.

4. Entrepreneurship is more important than innovation. The supply and demand is backward here: Almost all countries, states, and cities have bet everything on innovation. Innovation is critical, but it plays a supporting role to almighty entrepreneurship. The investments should follow rare entrepreneurs versus the worldwide oversupply of innovation. Put another way, it's far better to invest in entrepreneurial people than in great ideas.

5. America cannot outrun its healthcare costs. This is dead weight for the United States that virtually no other country carries. Every leader has to put physical fitness at the core of every decision he or she makes or surrender America's leadership of the free world. American managers need to review their teams on performance and growth but also on overall health and wellbeing.

6. The American public school dropout rate is approximately one-third — 50% among minorities. Because all public education results are local, local leaders need to lead their whole cities and all youth programs to war on the dropout rate with a strategy of one city, one school, one student at a

time. If they don't, they will lose jobs. The fate of a nation rides on the financial literacy and entrepreneurial energy of its kids.

7. The United States must differentiate itself by doubling its number of engaged employees. Disengagement and low-energy workplaces ultimately kill jobs. Only 28% of the American workforce is ready to compete and win each day. Doubling that number would change U.S. vs. China outcomes. Doubling it creates more customers, more jobs, and more startups and generally doubles the economic energy of the United States. Running a lousy workplace is now not only bad business, but it is also un-American.

8. Jobs occur where new customers appear. For that reason, the science of customers, often referred to as customer insight or customer centricity, is more important today than ever before. Customer centricity and deep customer insight are essential in this war. Americans have to understand global customers better than anybody else in the world does, or lose the competition for the next $140 trillion of global GDP growth.

9. Every economy rides on the backs of small to medium-sized businesses. So goes their state of mind, especially optimism and determination, so goes America's economic future. Most jobs occur when entrepreneurs start companies. The next

biggest job source is the approximately 5% of existing small companies that shoot up to big success. Cities have to create environments where this is highly encouraged, supported, mentored, and celebrated. Every strategy about everything has to relate to small-business creation and acceleration.

10. So go exports, so goes the coming jobs war. The United States needs to more than triple exports in the next five years and increase them by 20 times in the next 30 years. The U.S. cannot win the coming jobs war by just selling more products to its own consumers. The country has to export. Exporting is its next man-on-the-moon moment.

If the United States were to master these 10 demands, the country would not only reverse its predicted demise, but it would also create more global friendships based on the ultimate mutual respect from business partnerships. And when the smoke clears, the United States of America will have won its third world war through peaceful means — by winning the global jobs war.

Much of what I've written is grim, and many of the prescriptions are hard. I've even wondered if any of this is possible. But it is. AJ, the housekeeper's son, doesn't doubt for a minute that there will be a great job out there for him. Look at all the engaged workers in companies all over the world, working like there's no end to the possibilities in the economy around them. They aren't wrong. And if they continue like this, they won't fail.

But they can *be* failed. They can be failed with bad policies, wrong-headed social assumptions, mentors who don't connect, cities that collapse, kids who could have graduated, people who could have been healthy, worker engagement that could have been sparked but wasn't, and jobs that could have been created but weren't. When those workers are failed, countries fail too.

Failing the coming jobs war will be easy, and winning will be hard. Creating and keeping jobs will require a war. There will be no bystanders, but there will be victims. I don't want America to lose this war. This country is the beacon for the world's most talented people, the men and women who create the best jobs and continue to advance human development for the benefit of everyone.

The United States of America is an exceptional country with exceptional people. Once again, against the odds, she must rise up and win.

REFERENCES

Please note that any statistics not cited stem from Gallup research and/or studies.

Abouzeid, R. (2011, January 21). *Bouazizi: The man who set himself and Tunisia on fire*. Retrieved April 13, 2011, from http://www.time.com/time/world/article/0,8599,2043557,00.html

Adam Smith Institute. (n.d.). *The wealth of nations*. Retrieved April 12, 2011, from http://www.adamsmith.org/the-wealth-of-nations/

Al Gore Support Center. (n.d.). *Al Gore accomplishments (detailed list)*. Retrieved April 17, 2011, from http://www.algore2008.net/accomplishments2.html

Alam, M.S. (2011, January 13). A political murder in Pakistan or war? *Foreign Policy Journal*. Retrieved April 15, 2011, from http://www.foreignpolicyjournal.com/2011/01/13/a-political-murder-in-pakistan-or-war/

Alden, W. (2011, February 18). Illinois pension contribution plan "incredibly dangerous." *The Huffington Post*. Retrieved April 5, 2011, from http://www.huffingtonpost.com/2011/02/18/illinois-pension_n_824987.html

America's Promise Alliance. (n.d.). *Alliance partners*. Retrieved April 22, 2011, from http://www.americaspromise.org/Partnerships/Alliance-Partners.aspx

Americans continue to die from preventable injuries. (cover story). (2009). Worldwide Databases, *21*(9), 1-4. Retrieved from EBSCOhost.

Angner, E., & Loewenstein, G. (2006, November 20). *Behavioral economics*. Retrieved April 12, 2011, from http://sds.hss.cmu.edu/media/pdfs/loewenstein/BehavioralEconomics.pdf

Anheuser-Busch. (n.d.). *St. Louis brewing roots*. Retrieved April 21, 2011, from http://www.anheuser-busch.com/s/index.php/our-heritage/history/

Associated Press. (2010, February 18). Study: Michigan faces public employee pension gap. *The Oakland Press*. Retrieved April 5, 2011, from http://www.theoaklandpress.com/articles/2010/02/18/news/doc4b7d1e7d37fa8981623381.txt?viewmode=fullstory

Bainbridge, W.S. (Ed.). (2004). *Berkshire encyclopedia of human-computer interaction* (Vol. 2). Great Barrington, MA: Berkshire.

Bartlett, B. (2009, July 3). Health care: Costs and reform *Forbes*. Retrieved April 23, 2011, from http://www.forbes.com/2009/07/02/health-care-costs-opinions-columnists-reform.html

Barton, P.E. (2005). *One-third of a nation: Rising dropout rates and declining opportunities*. Retrieved April 22, 2011, from http://www.ets.org/Media/Education_Topics/pdf/onethird.pdf

BBC. (2011, February 8). *Profile: Egypt's Wael Ghonim*. Retrieved April 13, 2011, from http://www.bbc.co.uk/news/world-middle-east-12400529

Beamish, R. (2011 May 1). Back to school for the billionaires. *Newsweek*. Retrieved May 1, 2011, from http://www.newsweek.com/2011/05/01/back-to-school-for-the-billionaires.html

Belasco, A. (2011, March 29). *The cost of Iraq, Afghanistan, and other global war on terror operations since 9/11*. Retrieved May 24, 2011, from http://www.fas.org/sgp/crs/natsec/RL33110.pdf

Biographical Directory of the United States Congress. (n.d.). *Gore, Albert Arnold, Jr.* Retrieved April 17, 2011, from http://bioguide.congress.gov/scripts/biodisplay.pl?index=g000321

Biography.com. (n.d.). *Ted Turner Biography*. Retrieved April 18, 2011, from http://www.biography.com/articles/Ted-Turner-9512255

Bloomberg. (2009, August 1). *U.S. recession worst since great depression, revised data show*. Retrieved April 5, 2011, from http://www. bloomberg.com/apps/news?pid=newsarchive&sid=aNivTjr852TI

Brady, D. (2010, September 8). The challenges facing Burger King buyer 3G Capital. *BusinessWeek*. Retrieved April 21, 2011, from http://www.businessweek.com/magazine/content/10_38/ b4195018489726.htm

Brown, I.T., & Khoury, C. (2009, August 20). *In OECD countries, universal healthcare gets high marks*. Retrieved April 23, 2011, from http://www.gallup.com/poll/122393/oecd-countries-universal-healthcare-gets-high-marks.aspx

Buckingham, M., & Clifton, D.O. (2001). *Now, discover your strengths*. New York: Free Press.

Bureau of Labor Statistics. (n.d.). *The Employment Situation — June 2011*. Retrieved May 1, 2011, from http://www.bls.gov/news. release/pdf/empsit.pdf

Burger King. (n.d.). *About BK*. Retrieved April 21, 2011, from http:// www.bk.com/en/us/company-info/press/index.html

Campbell, A. (2006, October 16). *Partnering and strategic alliances — Resources for you*. Retrieved April 18, 2011, from http:// smallbiztrends.com/2006/10/partnering-and-strategic-alliances-resources-for-you.html

Cantril, H. (1965). *The pattern of human concerns*. New Brunswick, NJ: Rutgers University Press.

Cardenas, M., & Rozo, S. (2008). *Does crime lower growth? Evidence from Colombia*. Retrieved April 29, 2011, from http://www. growthcommission.org/storage/cgdev/documents/gcwp030web.pdf

Carroll, J. (2006, January 10). *Americans, Canadians, Britons similarly rate their healthcare systems*. Retrieved April 23, 2011, from http:// www.gallup.com/poll/20821/americans-canadians-britons-similarly-rate-their-healthcare-systems.aspx

Center for Research on Education Outcomes. (2009, June). *Multiple choice: Charter school performance in 16 states*. Retrieved April 21, 2011, from http://credo.stanford.edu/reports/MULTIPLE_ CHOICE_CREDO.pdf

Centers for Medicare & Medicaid Services. (n.d.). *National health expenditure 2009 highlights*. Retrieved April 23, 2011, from https://www.cms.gov/NationalHealthExpendData/downloads/ highlights.pdf

Centers for Medicare & Medicaid Services. (n.d.). NHE fact sheet. Retrieved April 23, 2011, from https://www.cms.gov/ NationalHealthExpendData/25_NHE_Fact_Sheet.asp

Central Intelligence Agency. (2011, April 9). *The world factbook*. Retrieved April 23, 2011, from https://www.cia.gov/library/ publications/the-world-factbook/index.html

Cerf, V.G., & Kahn, R.E. (1974, May). A protocol for packet network intercommunication. *IEEE Transactions on Communications*, *22*(5), 637-648.

Chantrill, C. (2011, April 8). *Total budgeted government spending.* Retrieved April 8, 2011, from http://www.usgovernmentspending. com/index.php

The Chubby Team. (2009, July 15). *Top cities for venture capital in Q2 '09 — New York and Seattle.* Retrieved April 15, 2011, from http:// www.chubbybrain.com/blog/top-cities-for-venture-capital-in-q2-2009-new-york-and-seattle/

Citgo. (n.d.). *Company history.* Retrieved April 21, 2011, from http:// www.citgo.com/AboutCITGO/CompanyHistory.jsp

Clifton, J. (2007). *Global migration patterns and job creation.* Omaha, NE: Gallup.

Clifton, J., & Marlar, J. (2011). *Good jobs: The new global standard.* Omaha, NE: Gallup.

CNN World. (1999, May 28). World's largest army not necessarily the strongest. Retrieved April 5, 2011, from http://articles.cnn. com/1999-05-28/world/9905_28_china.military_1_china-analyst-nuclear-arsenal-prime-minister-li-peng?_s=PM:WORLD

CNNMoney. (n.d.). *Fortune 500*. Retrieved April 18, 2011, from http://money.cnn.com/magazines/fortune/fortune500/2010/ full_list/101_200.html

Committee for Capitalizing on Science, Technology, and Innovation: An Assessment of the Small Business Innovation Research Program. (2009). *An assessment of the small business innovation research program at the department of defense.* Retrieved May 25, 2011, from http:// www.ncbi.nlm.nih.gov/books/NBK32835/pdf/TOC.pdf

Congress of the U.S., Senate Committee on Commerce, Science, and Transportation. (1991, March 5). High-performance computing and communications act of 1991. Retrieved April 17, 2011, from http://www.eric.ed.gov/PDFS/ED332694.pdf

Crane, D. (2010, April 6). California's $500-billion pension time bomb. *Los Angeles Times*. Retrieved April 5, 2011, from http:// articles.latimes.com/2010/apr/06/opinion/la-oe-crane6-2010apr06

Curry, S.R. (2011, March 2). *Warren Buffett: Buy affordable home, not your dream home.* Retrieved April 15, 2011, from http://realestate. aol.com/blog/2011/03/02/warren-buffett-buy-affordable-home-not-your-dream-home/?ncid=AOLCOMMre00sharartl0001

Daglis, I.A. (Ed.). (2001). *Space storms and space weather hazards.* Dordrecht, Netherlands: Kluwer.

De la Merced, M.J., & Maynard, M. Fiat deal with Chrysler seals swift 42-day overhaul. *The New York Times*. Retrieved April 21, 2011, from http://www.nytimes.com/2009/06/11/business/global/11chrysler.html

Deaton, A. (2008). Income, health, and well-being around the world: Evidence from the Gallup World Poll. *Journal of Economic Perspectives, 22*(2), 53-72.

Demott, J.S., & Byrnes, R. (1985, February 4). Here come the intrapreneurs. *TIME*. Retrieved April 18, 2011, from http://www.time.com/time/magazine/article/0,9171,959877,00.html

Discover. (2008, December). The "father of the Internet" would rather you call him "Vint." [Electronic version].

Don't Mess With Texas. (n.d.). *History: Don't mess with Texas*. Retrieved May 3, 2011, from http://dontmesswithtexas.org/history/

Editorials. (2005, May 31). CNN changed news — for better and worse. *Taipei Times*. Retrieved April 18, 2011, from http://www.taipeitimes.com/News/editorials/archives/2005/05/31/2003257358/1

Electronic Frontier Foundation. (n.d.). Gore bill. Retrieved April 17, 2011, from http://w2.eff.org/Net_culture/Net_info/Misc/gore.bill

Encyclopedia of Information Technology. (2007). New Delhi: Atlantic.

Federal Accounting Standards Advisory Board. (n.d.). *Authoritative source of guidance*. Retrieved April 20, 2011, from http://www. fasab.gov/accepted.html

Fin24. (2010, December 10). *Vavi: Beware of predatory elite*. Retrieved April 15, 2011, from http://www.fin24.com/Economy/Vavi-Beware-of-predatory-elite-20101210

Finkelstein, E.A., DiBonaventura, M.C., Burgess, S.M., & Hale, B.C. (2010). The costs of obesity in the workplace. *Journal of Occupational and Environmental Medicine, 52*(10), 971-976.

Flegal, K.M., Carroll, M.D., Ogden, C.L., & Curtin, L.R. (2010). Prevalence and trends in obesity among US adults, 1999-2008. *Journal of the American Medical Association, 303*(3), 235-241.

Fogel, R. (2010). $123,000,000,000,000. *Foreign Policy*, (177), 1. Retrieved May 24, 2011, from EBSCO*host*.

Gallup (n.d.). *Gallup daily: U.S. life evaluation*. Retrieved April 29, 2011, from http://www.gallup.com/poll/110125/Gallup-Daily-Life-Evaluation.aspx

Gallup. (2009). *The next discipline: Applying behavioral economics to drive growth and profitability*. Omaha, NE: Gallup.

Gallup. (2010). *State of the American workplace: 2008-2010*. Omaha, NE: Gallup

Gallup. (2010). *The state of the global workplace: A worldwide study of employee engagement and wellbeing.* Omaha, NE: Gallup.

Gallup. (2010, February 1). *Gallup employment classifications.* Omaha, NE: Gallup.

Gallup. (2011). *Building a more positive future for America's youth: Development and validation of the Gallup-Operation HOPE Financial Literacy Index.* Omaha, NE: Gallup.

Gallup. (2011, April 5). *Gallup global employment tracking.* Retrieved April 5, 2011, from http://www.gallup.com/poll/145487/Gallup-Global-Employment-Tracking.aspx

Gallup Management Journal. (2006, January 12). Gallup study: Feeling good matters in the workplace. *Gallup Management Journal.* Retrieved April 21, 2011, from http://gmj.gallup.com/content/20770/gallup-study-feeling-good-matters-in-the.aspx

Google, Inc. (2005, September 8). *Cerf's up at Google.* Retrieved April 15, 2011, from http://www.google.com/press/pressrel/vintcerf.html

Gray, S. (n.d.). *Detroit: 10 things to do in 24 hours.* Retrieved April 10, 2011, from http://www.time.com/time/travel/cityguide/article/0,31489,1994456_1994357_1994238,00.html

Gunther, M. (2006, October 4). *Ted Turner's Montana adventure.* Retrieved April 18, 2011, from http://money.cnn.com/2006/10/03/news/economy/pluggedin_gunther_bison.fortune/index.htm

Harter, J.K., Schmidt, F.L., Killham, E.A., & Agrawal, S. (2009, August). *Q¹² meta-analysis: The relationship between engagement at work and organizational outcomes*. Omaha, NE: Gallup.

Healey, J.R. (2009, February 25). Obama's auto faux pas leads to history lesson. *USA TODAY*. Retrieved April 18, 2011, from http://www.usatoday.com/money/autos/2009-02-25-obama-claim-daimler-differs_N.htm

Hoover, D.R., Crystal, S., Kumar, R., Sambamoorthi, U., & Cantor, J.C. (2002). Medical expenditures during the last year of life: Findings from the 1992-1996 Medicare current beneficiary survey. *Heath Services Research*, *37*(6), 1625-1642.

Hunt, Tristram. (2004, June 6). *One last time they gather, the greatest generation*. Retrieved April 10, 2011, from http://www.guardian.co.uk/uk/2004/jun/06/secondworldwar

Jacobe, D. (2011, March 31). *Gallup finds U.S. unemployment rate at 10.0% in March*. Retrieved April 5, 2011, from http://www.gallup.com/poll/146900/Gallup-Finds-Unemployment-Rate-March.aspx

Jacobs, D.G. (2005, September). Blockbuster growth. *SmartBusiness*. Retrieved April 18, 2011, from http://www.huizenga.nova.edu/About/BlockbusterGrowth.pdf

Jacobs, J. (2006, September 30). Award winning campaign comes from local roots. *Corsicana Daily Sun*. Retrieved May 2, 2011, from http://corsicanadailysun.com/local/x212332626/Award-winnng-campaign-comes-from-local-roots/print

Jones, J.M. (2010, November 30). *Americans prioritize deficit reduction as an economic strategy*. Retrieved April 8, 2011, from http://www.gallup.com/poll/144956/Americans-Prioritize-Deficit-Reduction-Economic-Strategy.aspx

Joyce, C.A. (Ed.). (2008). *The world almanac and book of facts*. New York: World Almanac.

Kanter, L. (1999, August 31). Warren Buffett. *Salon*. Retrieved April 15, 2011, from http://www.salon.com/people/bc/1999/08/31/buffett

Kelley, R. (2009, October). *Where can $700 billion in waste be cut annually from the U.S. healthcare system?* Retrieved April 23, 2011, from http://www.factsforhealthcare.com/whitepaper/HealthcareWaste.pdf

Keynes, J.M. (2006). *The general theory of employment, interest and money*. New Delhi: Atlantic.

Khoury, C., & Brown, I.T. (2009, March 31). *Among OECD nations, U.S. lags in personal health*. Retrieved April 23, 2011, from http://www.gallup.com/poll/117205/Americans-Not-Feeling-Health-Benefits-High-Spending.aspx

Kohn, L.T., Corrigan, J.M., & Donaldson, M.S. (2000). *To err is human: Building a safer health system.* Washington, D.C.: National Academy Press.

Langan, P.A., & Durose, M.R. (2004, October 21). *The remarkable drop in crime in New York City.* Retrieved April 29, 2011, from http://www.scribd.com/doc/322928/Langan-rel

Langlois, S. (2003, March 10). *Sleeping tight in Luxembourg.* Retrieved April 29, 2011, from http://www.marketwatch.com/ story/worlds-most-safe-dangerous-cities

Library of Economics and Liberty. (n.d.). *An inquiry into the nature and cause of the wealth of nations.* Retrieved April 12, 2011, from http://www.econlib.org/library/Smith/smWN.html

Lohr, S. (1993, August 24). I.B.M. said to focus on Intel clone. *The New York Times.* Retrieved April 18, 2011, from http://www.nytimes. com/1993/08/24/business/ibm-said-to-focus-on-intel-clone.html

Lopez, S.J. (2011). *Youth readiness for the future: A report on findings from a representative Gallup Student Poll sample.* Omaha, NE: Gallup.

Lopez, S.J., Agrawal, S., & Calderon, V.J. (2010, August). *The Gallup Student Poll technical report.* Omaha, NE: Gallup.

Lowrey, A. (2011, January 31). *Protesting on an empty stomach: How the Egyptian economy is fueling unrest in Egypt.* Retrieved April 13, 2011, from http://www.slate.com/id/2283217/

Marlar, J. (2010, March 9). *The emotional cost of underemployment.* Retrieved April 5, 2011, from http://www.gallup.com/poll/126518/Emotional-Cost-Underemployment.aspx

Marlar, J. (2010, March 9). *Six in 10 underemployed not hopeful about finding work.* Retrieved April 5, 2011, from http://www.gallup.com/poll/126122/Six-Underemployed-Not-Hopeful-Finding-Work.aspx

Mateja, J. (1999, January 7). Wayne Huizenga isn't your ordinary used-car salesman. *Chicago Tribune.* Retrieved April 18, 2011, from http://articles.chicagotribune.com/1999-01-07/business/9901070629_1_used-car-superstore-new-car-franchises-autonation

McCarthy, T. (1999, August 23). *Lee Kuan Yew.* Retrieved April 14, 2011, from http://www.time.com/time/world/article/0,8599,2054444,00.html

McHugh, J. (2010, May 7). Michigan pension fund shortfall: $11.5 billion, not $51.3 billion. *Mackinac Center for Public Policy.* Retrieved April 5, 2011, from http://www.mackinac.org/12703

McLean, B. (2011, February). Mr. Warren's confession. *Vanity Fair.* Retrieved April 15, 2011, from http://www.vanityfair.com/business/features/2011/02/warren-buffett-201102

Mehta, S. (2010, September 21). eBay founder won't endorse Meg Whitman for governor. *Los Angeles Times.* Retrieved April 18, 2011, from http://latimesblogs.latimes.com/california-politics/2010/09/ ebay-creator-pierre-omidyar-wont-endorse-meg-whitman-for-governor.html

Melville, K. (2006). *Learning to finish: The school dropout crisis.* Retrieved April 22, 2011, from http://www.pew-partnership.org/ pdf/dropout_overview.pdf

Mendes, E. (2010, February 9). *Six in 10 overweight or obese in U.S., more in '09 than in '08.* Retrieved April 23, 2011, from http:// www.gallup.com/poll/125741/Six-Overweight-Obese.aspx

Mendes, E. (2010, September 17). *Obesity linked to lower emotional wellbeing.* Retrieved April 23, 2011, from http://www.gallup.com/ poll/143045/Obesity-Linked-Lower-Emotional-Wellbeing.aspx

Mintz, S. (2007). *Digital history.* Retrieved April 5, 2011, from http://www.digitalhistory.uh.edu/database/article_display. cfm?HHID=188

Morales, L. (2010, October 15). *Americans disagree on how to fix entitlement programs.* Retrieved April 8, 2011, from http://www. gallup.com/poll/143705/Americans-Disagree-Fix-Entitlement-Programs.aspx

Mydans, S. (2007, August 29). *Lee Kuan Yew, founder of Singapore, changing with times.* Retrieved April 14, 2011, from http://www. nytimes.com/2007/08/29/world/asia/29iht-lee.1.7301669.html

National Center for Chronic Disease Prevention and Health Promotion. (2009). *The power of prevention: Chronic disease . . . the public health challenge of the 21ˢᵗ century.* Retrieved April 23, 2011, from http://www.cdc.gov/chronicdisease/pdf/2009-Power-of-Prevention.pdf

National Center for Health Statistics. (n.d.). *NCHS health e-stat.* Retrieved April 29, 2011, from http://www.cdc.gov/nchs/data/hestat/overweight/overweight_adult.htm

National Center for Health Statistics. (2007). *Health, United States, 2007: With chartbook on trends in the health of Americans.* Retrieved April 29, 2011, from http://www.cdc.gov/nchs/data/hus/hus07.pdf

National Park Service U.S. Department of the Interior. (n.d.). *Wright Brothers.* Retrieved April 17, 2011, from http://www.nps.gov/wrbr/index.htm

National Priorities Project. (n.d.) *Cost of war.* Retrieved May 4, 2011, from http://costofwar.com/en/

The New York Times. (2009, September 11). Health care abroad: France. *The New York Times.* Retrieved April 23, 2011, from http://prescriptions.blogs.nytimes.com/2009/09/11/health-care-abroad-france/

Newman, R. (2009, September 15). 4 countries with better healthcare than ours. *U.S. News & World Report.* Retrieved April 23, 2011, from http://money.usnews.com/money/blogs/flowchart/2009/09/15/4-countries-with-better-healthcare-than-ours-

News24. (2010, September 21). *ANC concerned about 'predatory elite.'* Retrieved April 15, 2011, from http://www.news24.com/SouthAfrica/Politics/ANC-concerned-about-predatory-elite-20100921

Nova Southeastern University. (n.d.). *H. Wayne Huizenga.* Retrieved April 18, 2011, from http://www.huizenga.nova.edu/About/HWayneHuizenga.cfm

Office of Management and Budget. (2011). *Budget of the U.S. government: Fiscal year 2011.* Retrieved April 8, 2011, from http://www.gpoaccess.gov/usbudget/fy11/pdf/budget.pdf

Office of the United States Trade Representative. (2010, January 19). *Weekly trade spotlight: Small and medium-sized enterprises: Overview of participation in U.S. imports.* Retrieved April 8, 2011, from http://www.ustr.gov/about-us/press-office/blog/2010/january/weekly-trade-spotlight-small-and-medium-sized-enterprises-ov

Operation HOPE. (n.d.). *Measuring the HOPE effect.* Retrieved April 22, 2011, from http://www.operationhope.org/index.cfm/act/Initiative/pid/8

Orfield, G., Losen, D., Wald, J., & Swanson, C.B. (2004). *Losing our future: How minority youth are being left behind by the graduation rate crisis.* Retrieved April 22, 2011, from http://www.urban.org/uploadedPDF/410936_LosingOurFuture.pdf

Palmeri, C. (2009, January 2). Worst recession since the 30s will end in 2009. *Bloomberg Businessweek.* Retrieved April 5, 2011, from http://www.businessweek.com/the_thread/hotproperty/archives/2009/01/worst_recession_since_the_30s_will_end_in_2009.html

Pappas, S. (2010, October 8). *Obesity's hidden job costs: $73 billion.* Retrieved April 29, 2011, from http://www.msnbc.msn.com/id/39571973/ns/health-diet_and_nutrition/

PBS. (1999). *Birth of the Internet.* Retrieved April 17, 2011, from http://www.pbs.org/transistor/background1/events/arpanet.html

PBS. (2004, December 21). *Fidel Castro.* Retrieved April 14, 2011, from http://www.pbs.org/wgbh/amex/castro/timeline/index.html

Pearson, M. (2009, September). *Disparities in health expenditure across OECD countries: Why does the United States spend so much more than other countries?* Retrieved April 23, 2011, from http://www.oecd.org/dataoecd/5/34/43800977.pdf

Pietrusza, D. (Ed.). (2008). *Silent Cal's Almanack: The Homespun Wit and Wisdom of Vermont's Calvin Coolidge.* Charleston: CreateSpace.

Prudential. (n.d.) *Understanding Social Security.* Retrieved May 2, 2011, from http://www3.prudential.com/signature/Social-Security.html

Rath, T., & Clifton, D.O. (2004, October 14). The big impact of small interactions. *Gallup Management Journal.* Retrieved April 12, 2011, from http://gmj.gallup.com/content/12916/big-impact-small-interactions.aspx

Rath, T., & Harter. J. (2010). *Wellbeing: The five essential elements.* New York: Gallup Press.

Ray, J. (2008, April 29). *China's leadership better regarded outside the west.* Retrieved April 8, 2011, from http://www.gallup.com/poll/106858/chinas-leadership-better-regarded-outside-west.aspx

Reeves, S. (2005, September 23). Caribou Coffee's robust IPO. *Forbes.* Retrieved April 21, 2011, from http://www.forbes.com/2005/09/23/cariboucoffee-IPO-equities-cx_sr_0923ipooutlook.html

Robison, J. (2008, April 10). What's next for banks? *Gallup Management Journal.* Retrieved April 14, 2011, from http://gmj.gallup.com/content/105988/whats-next-banks.aspx#1

Rosenberg, S. (2000, October 5). Did Gore invent the Internet? *Salon.* Retrieved April 15, 2011, from http://www.salon.com/technology/col/rose/2000/10/05/gore_internet

Ross, J. (2006). *Forward march.* Bloomington, IN: AuthorHouse.

Saad, L. (2008, July 24). *U.S. smoking rate still coming down.* Retrieved April 29, 2011, from http://www.gallup.com/poll/109048/us-smoking-rate-still-coming-down.aspx#2

Saad, L. (2011, February 14). *China surges in Americans' views of top world economy.* Retrieved April 5, 2011, from http://www.gallup.com/poll/146099/China-Surges-Americans-Views-Top-World-Economy.aspx

SBIR.gov. (n.d.). *About SBIR and STTR programs.* Retrieved May 25, 2011, from http://www.sbir.gov/about/index.htm

Schaper, D. (2010, March 24). Shortfall threatens Illinois pension system. *NPR.* Retrieved April 5, 2011, from http://www.npr.org/templates/story/story.php?storyId=125076655

Schulte, B. (2006, November 26). A Texas mess over coal. *U.S. News & World Report.* Retrieved May 3, 2011, from http://crosswords911.com/antilittering.jsp?q=aHR0cDovL3d3dy51c25ld3MuY29tL3Vzb mV3cy9uZXdzL2FydGljbGVzLzA2MTEyNi80Y29hbC5odG0=

Semega, J. (2009, September). *Median household income for states: 2007 and 2008 American Community Surveys.* Retrieved April 30, 2011, from http://www.census.gov/prod/2009pubs/acsbr08-2.pdf

Smith, C. (2011, February 28). Vinton Cerf, 'father of the Internet,' on the Internet's challenges. *The Huffington Post.* Retrieved April 15, 2011, from http://www.huffingtonpost.com/2011/02/26/vinton-cerf-future-of-the-internet_n_828322.html

Spain, W., & Goldstein, S. (2008, July 14). *Anheuser-Busch accepts $52 billion InBev offer*. Retrieved April 21, 2011, from http://www. marketwatch.com/story/anheuser-busch-accepts-52-billion

Spence, R.M. Jr. (2009). *It's not what you sell, it's what you stand for*. New York: Penguin.

St. Peter, A. (2010). *The greatest quotations of all-time*. Bloomington: Xlibris.

Stein, R.B. (1981). New York City's economy in 1980. *Quarterly Review, 6*(1), 1-7.

Stelfox, H.T., Palmisani, S., Scurlock, C., Orav, E.J., & Bates, D.W. (2006). The "to err is human" report and the patient safety literature. *Quality and Safety in Health Care, 15*, 174-178.

Stewart, B. (2000). *Vinton Cerf — TCP/IP co-designer*. Retrieved May 1, 2011, from http://www.livinginternet.com/i/ii_cerf.htm

Stockholm International Peace Research Institute. (April 2011). *Background paper on SIPRI military expenditure data, 2010*. Retrieved April 5, 2011, from http://www.sipri.org/research/ armaments/milex/factsheet2010

Stone, M. (1990, November 19). Hard Times. *New York, 23*(45), 36-45.

Stooke, K. (2010, May 18). *Masai warriors from Kenya visit Swindon*. BBC. Retrieved April 5, 2011, from http://news.bbc.co.uk/local/wiltshire/hi/people_and_places/arts_and_culture/newsid_8689000/8689973.stm

Sum, A., Khatiwada, I., McLaughlin, J., & Palma, S. (2009, October). *The consequences of dropping out of high school: Joblessness and jailing for high school dropouts and the high cost for taxpayers*. Retrieved April 21, 2011, from http://www.clms.neu.edu/publication/documents/The_Consequences_of_Dropping_Out_of_High_School.pdf

Tax Policy Center. (n.d.). *Who doesn't pay federal taxes?* Retrieved April 30, 2011, from http://www.taxpolicycenter.org/taxtopics/federal-taxes-households.cfm

Thaler, R.H. (1999). Mental accounting matters. *Journal of Behavioral Decision Making, 12*(3), 183-206.

3G Capital. (n.d.). *About 3G Capital*. Retrieved April 21, 2011, from http://3g-capital.com/about.html

Toch, T. (2010, July 6). Small schools are still beautiful. *The Hechinger Report*. Retrieved April 21, 2011, from http://hechingerreport.org/content/small-schools-are-still-beautiful_3485/

Trading Economics. (n.d.). *China GDP growth rate*. Retrieved April 5, 2011, from http://www.tradingeconomics.com/united-states/gdp-growth

Trading Economics. (n.d.). *Country ranking by gross domestic product (GDP) in billions of dollars.* Retrieved April 5, 2011, from http://www.tradingeconomics.com/World-Economy/GDP.aspx

Trading Economics. (n.d.). *United States GDP growth rate.* Retrieved April 5, 2011, from http://www.tradingeconomics.com/united-states/gdp-growth

Trading Economics. (n.d.). *United States gross domestic product (GDP).* Retrieved April 5, 2011, from http://www.tradingeconomics.com/united-states/gdp

U.S. Census Bureau. (n.d.). *Statistics about business size (including small business) from the U.S. Census Bureau.* Retrieved May 24, 2011, from http://www.census.gov/econ/smallbus.html

U.S. Census Bureau. (2008). *Statistics of U.S. businesses.* Retrieved April 19, 2011, from http://www.census.gov/econ/susb/

U.S. Census Bureau. (2010, June 15). *Back to school: 2010–2011.* Retrieved May 2, 2011, from http://www.census.gov/newsroom/releases/archives/facts_for_features_special_editions/cb10-ff14.html

U.S. Census Bureau. (2011, February 7). *School enrollment — social and economic characteristics of students: October 2009.* Retrieved April 22, 2011, from http://www.census.gov/population/www/socdemo/school/cps2009.html

U.S. Census Bureau. (2011, April 5). *U.S. & world populations clocks.* Retrieved April 5, 2011, from http://www.census.gov/main/www/popclock.html

U.S. Census Bureau. (2011, April 5). *World POP clock projection.* Retrieved April 5, 2011, from http://www.census.gov/ipc/www/popclockworld.html

U.S. Census Bureau. (2011, April 5). *World population by age and sex.* Retrieved April 5, 2011, from http://www.census.gov/ipc/www/idb/worldpop.php

US Debt Clock.org. (2011, April 8). *US federal spending.* Retrieved April 8, 2011, from http://www.usdebtclock.org/

U.S. Small Business Administration. (n.d.). *Advocacy small business statistics and research.* Retrieved April 8, 2011, from http://web.sba.gov/faqs/faqIndexAll.cfm?areaid=24

U.S. Small Business Administration. (n.d.). *Employer firms, establishments, employment, and annual payroll small firm size classes, 2007.* Retrieved April 8, 2011, from http://archive.sba.gov/advo/research/us_07ss.pdf

United States Department of Labor. (n.d.). *Small business in America.* Retrieved April 19, 2011, from http://www.dol.gov/odep/pubs/ek00/small.htm

United States Department of Labor. (2011, April 5). *Economic news release: Employment situation technical note*. Retrieved April 5, 2011, from http://www.bls.gov/news.release/empsit.tn.htm

United States Department of Labor (2011, April 5). *Latest numbers: Unemployment rate*. Retrieved April 5, 2011, from http://www.dol.gov/

Van Allen, S. (1999, December 29). *George Gallup, twentieth-century pioneer*. Retrieved April 5, 2011, from http://www.gallup.com/poll/3376/georgc-gallup-twentiethcentury-pioneer.aspx

The Washington Post. (n.d.). Faces of the fallen. *The Washington Post*. Retrieved April 29, 2011, from http://projects.washingtonpost.com/fallen/

Waste Management. (n.d.). *About us*. Retrieved April 18, 2011, from http://www.wm.com/about/index.jsp

Weagley, R.O. (2010, June 24). *One big difference between Chinese and American households: Debt*. Retrieved April 30, 2011, from http://blogs.forbes.com/moneybuilder/2010/06/24/one-big-difference-between-chinese-and-american-households-debt/

Weise, E. (2005, May 18). Medical errors still claiming many lives. *USA TODAY*. Retrieved April 29, 2011, from http://www.usatoday.com/news/health/2005-05-17-medical-errors_x.htm

Wessner, C.W. (Ed.) (2009). *An assessment of the SBIR program at the Department of Defense.* Washington, D.C.: National Academy Press.

Whitehouse.gov. (n.d.). *Promoting innovation, reform, and excellence in America's public schools.* Retrieved April 21, 2011, from http://www.whitehouse.gov/the-press-office/fact-sheet-race-top

Williams, J.M. (2000, September 20). How everyone benefits from assistive tech's greatest hits. *Bloomberg Businessweek.* Retrieved April 15, 2011, from http://www.businessweek.com/bwdaily/dnflash/sep2000/nf20000920_400.htm

Williams, R. (2009, June 7). *Tax facts: Why nearly half of Americans pay no federal income tax.* Retrieved April 15, 2011, from http://www.taxpolicycenter.org/UploadedPDF/412106_federal_income_tax.pdf

Williams, R. (2009, June 29). *Tax facts: Who pays no income tax?* Retrieved April 15, 2011, from http://www.taxpolicycenter.org/UploadedPDF/1001289_who_pays.pdf

Wills, G. (March/April 1999). Bully of the free world. *Foreign Affairs, 78*(2), 50-59.

Wilson, D., & Purushothaman, R. (2003, October 1). *Dreaming with BRICs: The path to 2050.* Retrieved April 9, 2011, from http://www2.goldmansachs.com/ideas/brics/book/99-dreaming.pdf

The World Bank. (April 2011). *World development indicators: 2011.* Retrieved April 5, 2011, from http://data.worldbank.org/data-catalog/world-development-indicators?cid=GPD_WDI

The World Bank Group. (2004). *Beyond economic growth student book: Gross domestic product (GDP).* Retrieved April 5, 2011, from http://www.worldbank.org/depweb/english/beyond/global/glossary.html#34

Yang, C. (2005, July 4). Vinton Cerf: On to "InterPlaNet protocol." *Bloomberg Businessweek.* Retrieved April 15, 2011, from http://www.businessweek.com/magazine/content/05_27/b3941022.htm

Zorn, E. (2007, March 5). Reality check: Al Gore and the Internet. *Chicago Tribune.* Retrieved April 15, 2011, from http://blogs.chicagotribune.com/news_columnists_ezorn/2007/03/reality_check_a.html

Zuck, R.B. (2009). *The Speaker's Quote Book.* Grand Rapids, MI: Kregel.

ACKNOWLEDGEMENTS

Jennifer Robison and Geoff Brewer turned what was one of the hardest things I have done in more than 40 years as an employee at Gallup into the most fun and exhilarating project of all. There were places where we were stuck, and it appeared to me our thinking and concepts weren't hanging together and that we should turn back . . . and then . . . bam. Because of them, we would break through. Thank God for Jennifer and Geoff or this material simply would not exist.

Geoff and Jennifer and our ringleader, Executive Publisher Larry Emond, and the whole Gallup Press enterprise are having runaway success. It was a privilege to work with them because when and if they choose to help you, you virtually always win. So thank you. I know your power firsthand.

I'd also like to thank this very good team for their hard work, long hours, and commitment to excellence: fact checker Trista Kunce, copy editor Kelly Henry, designer Beth Karadeema, and Gallup Press Associate Publisher Pio Juszkiewicz.

And there are a few other teams and individuals whose work has been critical to this book:

Gale Muller, Jon Clifton, and their whole World Poll team.

All Gallup-affiliated senior scientists, especially Ed Diener, Danny Kahneman, Angus Deaton, and Alan Krueger.

Ben Leedle and the Healthways team.

Roy Spence, for two huge ideas.

John Hope Bryant, for his relentless pursuit of the financial literacy of 5th through 12th graders.

Deepak Chopra, for his unique insights into global connectedness.

Jim Harter and Tom Rath, for leading the science of wellbeing.

Sarah Van Allen, for helping me with everything.

Connie Rath, Shane Lopez, and Jason Milton, for the Student Poll.

Gallup's job creation team: Todd Johnson, Shay Hope, Sangeeta Badal, Gerardo Aranda, and Jim Krieger.

My irrepressible global-politics mentor, the late Alec Gallup.

My mother, Shirley, and late father, Don.

And to the Gallup tribe, who impacts the whole world, a little to a lot, every day: Thank you.

ABOUT THE AUTHOR

Jim Clifton is Chairman and CEO of Gallup. His most recent innovation, the Gallup World Poll, is designed to give the world's 7 billion citizens a voice in virtually all key global issues. Clifton has pledged to continue this effort to collect world opinion for 100 years in 150 countries.

Under Clifton's leadership, Gallup has achieved a fifteen-fold increase in its billing volume and expanded Gallup from a predominantly U.S.-based company to a worldwide organization with 40 offices in 30 countries and regions.

Clifton is also the creator of The Gallup Path, a metric-based economic model that establishes the linkages among human nature in the workplace, customer engagement, and business outcomes. This model is used in performance management systems in more than 500 companies worldwide.

Clifton serves on several boards and is Chairman of the Thurgood Marshall College Fund. He has received honorary degrees from Jackson State, Medgar Evers, and Bellevue Universities. He lives in Washington, D.C., with his wife, Susan.

Gallup Press exists to educate and inform the people who govern, manage, teach, and lead the world's 7 billion citizens. Each book meets Gallup's requirements of integrity, trust, and independence and is based on Gallup-approved science and research.